UNTO ALL THE WORLD; BOLD MISSION

Grady C. Cothen

Introduction by
Albert McClellan

BROADMAN
Nashville, Tennessee

Dedication

To Bettye
who taught me
the meaning of love

4255-08
ISBN: 0-8054-5508-6
Dewey Decimal Classification: 269
Subject heading: BOLD MISSION THRUST//WITNESSING

Library of Congress Catalog Card Number: 79-50341
Printed in the United States of America

Preface

This small volume is a personal statement and was born in the heat of the event—Bold Mission. It does not propose to be a carefully reasoned rationale for scholars or a systematic theology of missions. It is not an official statement for anyone. These statements come from the excitement of the long days and nights in the meetings, on the airplanes, in the planning and the confrontations.

I could hope that you might feel the urgency of it all as we have felt it. I hope that you can sense the seriousness of the issue as we did in the birth pangs of the unified effort. Perhaps you, too, will feel the drama of the brief and often criticized meeting conducted in the White House where God breathed a new dimension into our mission effort.

It would be pleasing if you could read it with the same sense of divine guidance for yourself that gripped those involved in the development of the plans for Bold Mission. It was as though God embraced the people and bore them along in the flood of his purpose.

God used many people in these preliminary stages, as he must use millions to execute the plans developed. I have been impressed with the response of the Southern Baptist Convention Executive Committee, for I have seen them in action.

I will name no persons, lest any person get credit for what God has done. If God has used people, that is his purpose, method, and will. That is enough. I am grateful he let me watch Bold Mission being born.

Acknowledgments

I gratefully acknowledge all those Baptist friends from coast to coast who played very important parts by listening to me expound many of these views which are written herein.

Gomer Lesch did considerable editorial work on this book. *Violet Medlin* typed most of it in one form or another, and those unnamed servants of the Lord in the *Word Processing Center* of the Baptist Sunday School Board typed and retyped portions of it. Albert McClellan wrote the Introduction.

Bettye was patient as usual while I lived it and tried to write it. To all these and others, I acknowledge my debt and express my gratitude!

GRADY C. COTHEN

Contents

Introduction

When I was quite young I was stirred by the phrase, "The power of an idea." I thought if I could just get the right idea I would have the power to change the world. But no idea came that seemed to hold the promise of the future.

They never do. The most pregnant ideas at first seem empty and foolish. Sometimes the best ideas are discarded because they appear sterile and impossible. About the only way a person can really recognize a good idea is to view it historically. Looking back a person can see its budding, its flowering, and its fruit—or lack of it—and know that what was first a suggestion has become a reality.

Bold Mission Thrust is such an idea. It may have originated in 1966 in a meeting of the '70 Onward Steering Committee, for it was from that meeting that a ten-year emphasis on "Sharing Christ" originated. The last two years were designated "Sharing Christ's Bold Mission."

As this writer remembers it, one of the first to speak the phrase was Marie Mathis of the

Woman's Missionary Union of the Southern Baptist Convention. Other mission leaders in the meeting were Elaine Dickson of the WMU, George Euting of the Brotherhood Commission, Arthur Rutledge, Fred Moseley and John Havlik of the Home Mission Board, and Harold Basden of the Foreign Mission Board. Elaine Dickson strongly supported Mrs. Mathis, as did some of the men present.

Without our really realizing the power of the idea, Bold Mission was born and destined to grow into what may be in our lifetime a significant Baptist event. It may be, as Leonard Irwin of the Home Mission Board said, "the greatest thing in my lifetime since I was born again."

Bold Mission was a concept approved by the Southern Baptist Convention in 1970. The Home Mission Board quietly began working to give it definite meaning in its cooperative relationships with state conventions. In a few years the HMB program emerged as BOLD MISSION THRUST—Acts 1:8. Following the Home Mission Board lead, many of the state conventions adopted it as the major thrust of their programs for the years 1977–1979.

Meanwhile, the idea of Bold Mission was growing in other places in Southern Baptist life. A special Committee of Fifteen was appointed by the SBC Executive Committee to study the work of the agencies in the denomination. One of its recommendations called for a major study of mission strategy. In response, the Convention appointed a Missions Challenge Committee (1974) that came forward with a proposal:

> That the Convention set as its primary missions challenge that every person in the world shall have the opportunity to hear the gospel of Christ in the next twenty-five years, and that in the presentation of this message, the biblical faith be magnified so that all men, women, and children can understand the claim Jesus Christ has on their lives. (1976)

The mustard-seed idea born ten years before had become a full-grown plant. Southern Baptists had at last made a latter day recommitment to the Great Commission. A year later, with Home Mission Board consent, the term "Bold Mission Thrust" was applied to a long-term emphasis which will run to the year 2000. It was also adopted as the theme for the three-year Convention program for 1979-1982.

ALBERT MCCLELLAN

Reprinted from *The Baptist Program,* October, 1978. © Copyright 1978, Southern Baptist Convention Executive Committee. Used by permission.

1
People in Panic

Several months ago, my wife and I were touring New Delhi, India, where we had stopped for a few days to satisfy my lifelong intellectual curiosity about the people. We engaged in conversation with a man who fancied himself a Hindu philosopher. I do not know much about Hinduism, but I question whether he was a Hindu philosopher. All the same, he posed as one.

I attempted to ask him about the religion of the Hindus, not from the theoretical, academic, or theological points of view, but from the perspective of the practitioners who lived with it and the consequences day by day in their lives.

We had seen the gods, the temples, and the shrines everywhere. We had seen them practice their faith, which to us seemed odd and bizarre, and yet to them seemed extremely important. We had watched them wash in the sacred river as they tried to find closer fellowship with God and relief from their sins. And as this man described to me the nature of their religious experience, he said, "You understand that the reincarnation is the curse, and that the people in their lives are attempting to avoid being reincarnated, especially in some lower form because of the deeds that they have done in this life. They're trying to find, at last, peace, so that it is the end of that endless cycle of life, misery, dying, and death—starting all over again in some other form, in some other person, even in some animal."

"But," he said, "once we get past the idols and the need for the shrines and the need for external evidences of religion, true Hinduism turns one's eyes inward upon oneself. When at last you can have self-contemplation only, you alone become important."

I do not know whether that communicates an adequate representation of Hinduism, either in its esoteric forms or in its academic expression. It seems a kind of bootstrap religion in which one thinks and acts his way out of the curse that leads to inevitable and eternal reincarnation. And it leads to the greatest of sin, if I understand the New Testament at all. For I believe the New Testament teaches that self-enthronement is the essence of idolatry and is the crucial nature of sin itself. We do not need to visit India and listen to the Hindu talk about his expression of religion to see evidences of self-enthronement.

As we look at the people to whom we carry Bold Mission, we see that self-centeredness and self-enthronement are manifest in the United

States and around the world. It is often expressed, "Do your own thing." Some years ago, a man I had known for many years was making a choice about the course of his life. He was about to do something that neither one of us believed was the right thing to do. Yet, he said to me, "I'm just going to be myself." And what he was about to do in order to be himself was the essence of the denial of the Christian faith.

Many times the cult of self-awareness seems to lead to idolatry. One could hope that we might soon be past the stage when people spend their entire lives trying to become aware of themselves to the exclusion of the rest of the world—and to the exclusion even of their own families. The cult of self is everywhere and is taking on enormous religious significance in our land. It is a national mania, this cult of self, that centers the expression of life on achieving the desires of the individual.

When we begin looking at the nature of the people to whom we must take the Word of God, we must be aware of inevitably running hard into the kind of idolatry, the enthronement of self, that says, "God is not for me. I am my own god, and I am my own determinant." This has already, as we shall see later, resulted in the fragmentation of society into literally thousands of small single-interest groups.

This enthronement of self is rooted intellectually in many different places. *Naturalism,* in my judgment, is often confused with science and is frequently taught in the high schools and universities as being science. Naturalism is that philosophy which teaches there is no transcendent reality. Reality is what you can see, feel, and touch, what you can taste, hear, and smell; that is the totality of reality, according to naturalism.

Naturalism says, "There is no God." It tells us man is not a product of creation but simply a product of the evolutionary process, and may be a higher result of the process. In naturalism there is no transcendent reality because there is no God. Because there is no transcendent reality, there is therefore no final accountability.

This philosophy teaches that there is no spiritual nature *per se*. It is a figment of man's need or of his higher imagination. And since man has no accountability, true reality is what you see and experience in your life. This has produced great sickness and untold misery as mankind has again and again come to the place where it says: "If there is no eternity, if I am only an animal, if there is no accountability, if there is no transcendent reality, if there is no God, why bother about it at all? Eat, drink, and be merry, for tomorrow you will be worm bait." And that, they claim, is the totality of reality!

This philosophy is vagrant in its forms and migrating in its influence until its tentacles spread into every facet of American life. For example, if you wonder why the arts have suddenly taken on such license, it is because they are rooted frequently in the philosophy that whatever is natural is acceptable. Whatever is natural and whatever is reality should control the way life ought to be lived. So pornography, homosexuality, adultery, fornication, lying, stealing, and all the rest is simply doing what comes naturally. These patterns of conduct as explained by moderns have their roots in the philosophy of naturalism.

There are various forms of *determinism* which seem to have their intellectual roots in the philosophy of naturalism. Sociological determinism says that if you're born into a set of adverse circumstances, you are the product of that society in which you live. And in all likelihood, unless you are an extraordinary individual, that society will control and mold you into a person who is the result of the determining factors of this life. If you are born in adverse circumstances, this philosophy purports, you will become the product of who your parents were, the food you ate, the society in which you grew up, the streets in which you fought, and the circumstances which surround your life.

This is, of course, antithetical to the Christian faith, which declares that man can rise above the level of the natural and is much more than animal. Man can be the son of the eternal God. He has a choice in life. But the human family is being decimated by godless naturalism, out of which grow various aspects of determinism.

The Christian faith says you can help what you are, if you understand that there is more to life than the physical—if you understand that there is more to reality than that which can be experienced by the five senses.

If there was ever a time in the history of the human family when the so-called perfectibility of man should have been destroyed for the myth it is, it ought to be now. This is the era of the greatest accumulation of knowledge in the history of man. Yet the grossest evil is manifest everywhere. This is the day when the greatest of scientific discoveries should have made possible Utopia on this earth, but selfish men still use the discoveries for themselves and for their own interests.

This is a time when education is disseminated in a fashion never before known to the human race, yet at this moment we are giving high school graduates exams to find out whether they can read, write, add, and subtract.

Here and now in an educated society with amazing technological expertise, we are plagued, beset, cursed, tried, and trampled by the nature of man who has not yet found purpose for life through Jesus Christ.

These are the people to whom we go. All of these things I have emphasized are in violation of the divine purpose. You see, God made man for himself, not to consume the divine blessings upon his own selfishness, but to relate in fellowship with God, and thus to relate eternally as the servant of his fellowman.

God made us for noble and eternal ends. God made us to be more than just animals. God made us to do more than spend the precious substance of life on trivia. It is, of course, a great tragedy that people are committing terrible sins. It is also a grievous tragedy of our land that so many people are piddling away their days and nights, the precious substance of life, on trivia that does not make any difference in the final analysis. God intended man to be like Him, and self-enthronement has awful consequences.

As I consider people in panic, I shall never forget the first time I took off at night in a small plane. It was at the southern end of the Los Angeles basin. There sparkled below the lights representing eight million people. The night was clear. The fog had not yet come in from the sea, and down below the car lights flowed in an endless river down the freeways. The people were crowded together in the houses like some crowded and complex ants' nest. By the time I crossed the Hollywood hills, the entire earth beneath me was ablaze with the lights of millions. As far as one could see, to the edge of the sea, north to the mountains, east to the barren desert, and south to the verdant hills, there were people.

The millions intimidated me. I couldn't count the millions. I couldn't empathize with the millions. But I do have some photographs of individual people in my mind, from which I shall never escape.

I have a mental photograph of my grandson who is probably the "world's champion salamander catcher." One afternoon at the Ridgecrest

Conference Center, he brought a whole bucket-ful to me in my room. While I was visiting him in Miami about four years ago, he brought one of his friends to see me. My grandson has hair that's almost blond, eyes that are blue, and fair skin. And he has those freckles we love, across the bridge of his nose and on his cheeks. Of course, he is the apple of our eye.

The friend he introduced me to was very black. His hair was straight. He was a beautiful child. His eyes looked at me as though they were the residual pools of human misery, coagulated in the personality of a child.

I looked at that beautiful young boy, and my grandson said, "Grandpa, I want you to meet Malcolm." Instinctively I stuck out my hand to shake hands with Malcolm, but Malcolm didn't understand what I was trying to do. It dawned on me that he didn't know how to shake hands, so I said, "Give me five, Malcolm!" He knew how to do that, and he "gave me five."

I watched Malcolm. He sat in a corner and didn't utter a sound. As my son-in-law moved around and as I moved around, Malcolm's eyes fastened on us like those of a cat, and every word we spoke he heard and every move we made he watched. And I perceived that here was a child hungry for relationships, who had a deep need in his life. Before I thought, trying to draw him out and get him to speak, I said, "Malcolm, what does your daddy do?" That, of course, is a traditional question you ask a child in trying to engage him in conversation.

But he looked at me with the fire of hell in his eyes, and almost spat it out at me. "Me don't got no daddy." And I could have cut my tongue out for putting him on the spot. I was embarrassed for the child, and the child was mortified, and that's the last word I heard Malcolm speak.

But I've thought of Malcolm a thousand times since. Oh, God, if somebody doesn't love him and reach out to him and encompass him and help him and witness to him and woo him by the power of God, he doesn't have a chance in this world. For the world cries to us, "You're just another animal—you'll never rise above the circumstances of your life."

But God answers, "Him that cometh to me I will in no wise cast out" (John 6:37, KJV). "Come unto me," God further says, "all ye that labour and are heavy laden, and I will give you rest" (Matt. 11:28, KJV).

That's the job God has called us to do—not to make more Baptists. Not to create more denominational statistics, but to let the love of God be demonstrated in the showcase of a human heart.

One early step toward reaching the monumental Bold Mission goal is to become sensitized to the needs of individuals. Too often we rationalize our spiritual inactivity—our failure to bear fruit—by grumbling that the task is impossible, the world too large, the multitudes too inaccessible.

We ignore the fact that Christ's commission was not a call to mass evangelism only, but to one-on-one witnessing. We shroud ourselves in a cloak of timidity, fear, and frustration at the magnitude of the assignment. In so doing, we betray the confidence of the One who promised, and delivered, the power of the Holy Spirit to each of his faithful followers.

What then of the man across the back fence, the children next door, the lonely old couple across the street? They may be whole and healthy spiritually and physically, but the probability is that they share at least a measure of the problems we all seem to bear in some degree.

Three characteristics, we are told by researchers, epitomize Americans today. The first of these is a sense of purposelessness. Multitudes have no sense of purpose for their lives. There is a sense of inner emptiness. Hosts of people are slogging through life with nothing internal that really satisfies their deep longings. There is a sense of hopelessness. The second leading cause of death among those between the ages of 11 and 24 is suicide! Hosts of Americans have no hope for now, for the future, or for eternity.

There are social forces at work today which are radically altering the nature of the people to whom we must minister. The work ethic, for example, has been supplanted by the "spirit of entitlement"—the attitude of "I deserve it. I have a right to it. It belongs to me as an integral part of my experience." Here is an emerging attitude which is going to vastly color the appeal we make on behalf of Christ.

We are deep into a time when we expect the government or the church or the school or some-one to remove the element of risk from life. And when the element of risk is removed, little progress is possible.

Return to determinism for a moment. We live in a time of social and psychological determinism which fosters irresponsibility. One of the most crucial elements of the social structure in our time is that vast numbers of people believe they are not responsible for themselves. They are not responsible for their families, and they have no responsibility to society. This loss of a sense of responsibility and of accountability makes it enormously more difficult to convince people that they ought to participate constructively in what the church is doing.

People now have no sense of accountability to their own families—no sense that the family can hold them personally responsible for what they do. Little sense of accountability to society. Little sense of accountability to the church.

When one puts into perspective that backdrop of sociological change, and measures it alongside the motivation of Christian loyalty, you are apt to be, as Dr. J. B. Gambrell used to say, "barkin' up a tree where there ain't no coon." The coon has come down from that tree. These and other factors have produced a fragmentation of society.

This fragmentation has been termed the "cult

of personalization." We are splintered into countless pressure groups, each of which is completely dedicated to its single narrow purpose, with no sense of responsibility or accountability to the public at large, no interest in the home or community. Congress has come almost to the place where it cannot take constructive social action in the passing of Federal statutes because of the multiplicity of pressure groups which want only what they consider important while the values of other people and groups are considered irrelevant and unimportant.

One report states that there are nineteen single-issue caucuses in the United States Congress. The number grows each year. There are the ethnic groups: black, Hispanic, the Ad Hoc Congressional Committee for Irish Affairs; and the geographical lineups: Great Lakes Senators, Northeast-Midwest Congressional Coalition, New England Congressional Caucus, Suburban Caucus, Rural Caucus, and the Port Caucus.

There are the economic interests: the Steel Caucus, Blue-Collar Caucus, Textile Caucus, Congressional Solar Coalition; and the research and watchdog groups: Environmental Study Conference, Members of Congress for Peace Through Law, Democratic Study Group, and the Congressional Clearing House on the Future.

And so the democratic process of compromise becomes more difficult, and the congressional process more volatile, according to *U.S. News and World Report* (January 22, 1979).

All of this together tells us that the sense of sacrifice has been lost from American life. People, the researchers report, are no longer willing to sacrifice for the family. By extension, we recognize that there will not be, then, sacrifice for church or for country. Some military leaders fear that we dare not become involved in another war of any description for fear that the sense of sacrifice is so absent from our society that we may not be able to defend ourselves. This may be extreme, but these trends can be substantiated by hard data—actual head counts and percentages—and they have been studied now for a period of eight years.

There are some other interesting studies of people in panic. For example, we know of the widespread interest in religious cults, in the guru, in mysticism. Twenty-seven percent of the American population believe that yoga can make life better, while only 16 percent believe that revivalism (Pentecostalism) can make life better. And the same number, 16 percent, believe that vegetarianism can make life better. Old-time religion? No, a new look, indeed.

How about other trends? Only 21 percent of the American public would like to see a return to the more traditional standards in sexual relationships. Fifty-four percent believe that there is nothing wrong with a couple living together without marriage if they care for each other. Another study places this figure at 57 percent of American men. Yet 77 percent would like a return to respect for other people's property. We want a return to some old ways but not to marital fidelity—but perhaps to basic honesty. Here is the mixed fruit of the thesis of naturalism, which chants "whatever is natural is good."

In America, we are interested in a religion that is taking strange and interesting and sometimes bizarre turns in form. It is often a religion without commitment to the ethical and moral principles of the Scriptures. As this begins to sink into the lower levels of consciousness and becomes determinant in the proclamation of the gospel, we will not be able to do it in the "same old way" any longer. We must come at it with many different approaches.

The approach of the basketball coach at Louisiana College, Billy Allgood, is a good way—the traditional way. "When I contact a prospect for the team," he says, "I inform him of the school's standards and tell him there are four priorities I am looking for.

"The first is his family and family relationships; the second is his religious commitment; the third is an allegiance to the school; and the fourth is a dedication to athletics."

Here is an adherence to traditional values that is to be praised. The Billy Allgoods of our time will do much to turn the trends I have mentioned toward the right direction. But thousands more like Allgood, *and* approaches that are as creative as the imagination can contrive, are needed to reverse the strange and mysterious forces that work among us today.

The old-time religion has a new look, and we are clearly called to accomplish the Bold Mission to which we have so soberly pledged ourselves.

There are other readily observable realities to consider as we reach out toward a people in panic.

Have you noticed in these latter years, particularly, the enormity of the pressures under which many people seem to be laboring? Everybody seems out of breath, chasing madly here and there, wondering *why* when they arrive at their destination. And they wonder if the trip is the meaning of the entire affair rather than the event that brought them there.

Then there are the pressures that rise out of the economic circumstances of life—the pressures of inflation. Who can keep up with it or anticipate it? We have economic pressures that are being brought on by the energy crunch, by the problems that are related to keeping warm or cool or traveling.

These economic pressures are arising out of the very fabric of the society in which we live, for we are no longer able to control the economics of the world. We are now one of the "have-not" nations related to the production of energy and a lot of other things. The economic pressures close in on every one of us. They make us wonder if we're going to be able to keep our heads above water.

The worried frowns, the crow's feet around the eyes, and the involuntary flinches of the cheeks and lips give evidence that America lives under tremendous stress. Some of it is economic, but much of it concerns the family. Much of it centers around the family for a hundred reasons—a hundred circumstances which we are unable to control.

Problems arise from working mothers or working wives. I do not criticize them! In some cases it is absolutely essential, an attempt by sincere persons to solve the economic pressures to which we have already referred. In other cases it contributes to the well-being of the family. And yet, pressures arise all the same. I have always thought that the mother of two children must have some special endowment from God to raise them, portraying love, and doesn't become totally unhinged before they are grown! I take my hat off to these mothers. *I* don't have what it takes to accomplish it! But think of the mother who works forty hours a week, tries to raise a family, and keep her husband happy in the process! Think of the stress!

Think of problems that are related to the family in the transmission of values. When I was growing up, if my mother were not home, I knew she was one of two places. She was either at church or the grocery store. She never went anywhere else, unless I was perfectly well aware of it. And some will say, "What a limited family!" Yes, I'm quite sure that's true, but there never was any question in my mind about where my mother was going to be, and how she was going to react to the circumstances of my life. There was the psychological cushion against which I could lean, absolutely certain that if I came in with a broken arm, stubbed toe, or hurt feelings, she was going to be there to help.

Wonderful were the values I was taught there. For my mother took endless time in teaching me what was right and wrong. She put up with my boyish nonsense, though sometimes she applied the "board of education" to the "seat of knowledge" to make a lasting impression. But she was always there. And it must be difficult for those who do not have this assurance.

There are pressures on the family structure, for very often there is no extended family unit. It used to be that if the mother wasn't there, grandma was, and grandpa was puttering around, and the family values were thus transmitted. I can remember my uncles, aunts, and cousins who tried to help my parents in the difficult times. There was cohesion in that extended family unit that is missing from so much of American society today.

I have cousins now that I wouldn't know if I were to meet them on the street. I must confess with shame that I do not even know if some of my uncles and aunts are still alive, for our lives have gone in different directions, and I do not have the support of that extended family unit.

We experience the pressures of the so-called new morality that is as old as Sodom and Gomorrah. But nowadays on television, adultery is made to appear romantic, and homosexuality is glorified or laughed at. It is no wonder that children cannot separate their values and know which are worthy and honorable. There are many pressures on the family unit.

Have you noticed recently how books, periodicals, radio, and television suggest that marriage is a transient institution to be destroyed at will, or any time a "meaningful relationship" can be established with somebody else? It's no wonder that we're raising a whole generation of emotionally unstable people who have no reason to be stable, for nothing about their lives stays stationary for very long.

We are experiencing a new kind of rootlessness. Have you noticed how many of us are trying to trace our family tree? We feel rootless because of the instability of the family; rootless because the public school systems too often are the instruments of social change rather than education. It is a curious phenomenon that states have to pass laws which require high school graduates to be able to read and write before they can get a diploma. The public school systems which used to be the transmitters of our values are now forbidden to do so by the law.

The social structures that used to tell us what

was right and wrong are now gone. And there is a kind of human reaction to all of this that makes us restless and uneasy, and there isn't any psychological bumper that we can brush up against in order to be steered back into the middle. It's no wonder that there is such a rootlessness in American society in our time.

Our reactions to all of this are rather interesting. Reactions such as escapism, which may take the form of alcohol or drugs or any kind of pleasure-seeking. Isn't it absolutely phenomenal that a basketball player makes two or three times the salary (in one year) of the president of the United States? It's a curious kind of phenomenon, and yet I like to watch basketball on television because it gives me a moment of peace and quiet when I can get away from all the realities of life. For when I see somebody seven-feet two-inches tall dunk the ball, I live vicariously, and I've forgotten for a moment all of my troubles. That's all right, provided we do not try to live out our lives escaping the reality of the world in which we live.

In strange and wondrous ways we Americans try to find some understanding, to put the pieces together in order to make sense of it all. We wander aghast in a world we do not understand, restless and uneasy, confused and bewildered. If you think we Christians have troubles, you ought to look at your friends who aren't Christians, who are searching in all the wrong places for all the wrong things, who are putting high values on those things which are transient, who are giving themselves away to causes that have no substance, and who are spending their lives on that which does not endure.

When the Bible says, "God created man in his own image," it knows precisely of what it speaks. Translate it into the language of our time. A person made with an appetite for the Bread of life cannot be satisfied spiritually with low-cal trash foods. A person in whom God created the appetite for the water of eternal life will never be satisfied with artificially-sweetened powdered drink. A person whom God made for the eternal affairs of the universe will never find fulfillment keeping up with the Joneses. And a person whom God made for heaven will be restless and uneasy at the prospects of hell. God made us in his image so that our spirits, minds, and needs would never be satisfied with anything short of God's eternal purpose for us. God made us for eternity.

How can we maintain our stability, understand our reactions, and come to grips with the harshness of the world we live in? How can we, in the face of the values of the world that are antithetical to what we believe—that are diametrically opposed to those which the Scriptures teach—how can we come to grips with the realities and truths of God and live in an alien society? This is puzzling until we remember that the Lord said, "If they persecuted me, they will persecute you. . . . He who hates me hates my Father also" (John 15:20,23). And a Christian who is at home in the social structures of this society is not living very close to God, for we are aliens and foreigners in a land where the principal values are things. Money, escapism, selfishness, and those values that cannot endure—How does all of this relate to us?

The more we know about the Word of God, and the closer we walk with him in its truths, the more we are alienated from many of the values of the society in which we live. Let's understand this and become comfortable with it. We can never, as Christians, be at ease with the kinds of moral structures which have been created on every side, and yet they tempt us.

We can never be satisfied with keeping up with the Joneses, and yet if we are not careful, we will spend the precious substance of life doing exactly that—trying to get the long car, the longer boat, the bigger airplane, the larger house, and the bigger bank account, and a long list of investments.

One of the reasons there are so many miserable Christians is that we have one foot in heaven and one foot in the world, and we are pulled between the societies we must live in. And the more we migrate toward God, the less at home in the world we are. The more we migrate toward the world, obeying its impulses and responding to its demands, the less at home with God we are, and the more miserable we are inside. There lies the dilemma.

Are we citizens of the kingdom of God or do we try to hold on to all the world and have the best of both worlds? I am absolutely convinced that the answers are not to be found in the philosophies of this world. The answers are to be found in the truths of God and his Word. Let us come back to the Word, and let us unashamedly confess it. Let us acknowledge it before the whole world. Having acknowledged it, having paid lip service to it, having resolved intellectually and spiritually that these are the answers and that they are to be found in the Word of God, is not enough.

There are not enough preachers and missionaries under the call of God to do the work God needs done in the world in our time. It thus becomes the business of believers in Jesus Christ, the church on Sunday as it is gathered. On Monday, it becomes the business of the church members to be the carriers of the truth of God.

You, not just the preachers or the missionaries, but *all* of the believers in Christ, as you go into the world, *you* "shall be my witnesses." The cruciality of the issue is the church, *you*. The form of the word we use for church is not found in the New Testament at all. The word for church in the New Testament always involves the people of God. The people! And the people of God— as part and parcel of the human family—must witness and minister to a people in panic.

2
Conflict or Conciliation

"Unto all the world" is more than a cliché that has, to use another cliché, seen better days. It is more than a book title. Much more.

It is so much more that it nearly defies articulation. It is an acknowledgment that the world has need of a message from those of us who call ourselves Christians. It is an admission that the people of the world have overwhelming needs, live under merciless pressures, and spend hours, days, dollars, and energies in frustrated seeking for an elusive, fog-shrouded, distant safe harbor toward which they may chart their course.

"Unto all the world" is an acknowledgment and an admission. It is also a dream and a challenge. The dream has been nurtured in the hearts of Christians since Jesus spoke—and lived—the Great Commission. "Go, then, to all peoples everywhere and make them my disciples: baptize them in the name of the Father, the Son, and the Holy Spirit, and teach them to obey everything I have commanded you. And I will be with you always, to the end of the age" (Matt. 28:19-20, TEV).

Southern Baptists are dreaming this dream afresh today, even as others in Christendom sharpen their witnessing skills and make similar commitments to evangelistic efforts. We, as a denomination, have accepted the first-century challenge. The challenge of committing human and financial resources to the twentieth-century emphasis in an unprecedented effort.

In the last decade many of us have ducked our heads and half closed our eyes while the world teetered on the brink of disaster. We have lived in a time when the nuclear weapons that may produce the ultimate holocaust have been put on alert by nations afraid of each other.

The university campuses, which are supposed to be the bastions of learning, became battlegrounds in fact instead of in symbol. Our society is fragmented into a thousand small interest groups which do not seem interested in each other or any other group.

Morals have been democratized so that whatever the majority wants becomes the norm. Moral and ethical judgments have become relative, and the norms of right and wrong have given way to hedonism. Humanism has been substituted for the Christian faith, and some denominations have publicly declared that they have no message to commend to other religions and cultures.

Amid all of this, Southern Baptists propose

an interesting, frightening, challenging, and so-bering effort called "Bold Mission Thrust." We have declared that we will preach the gospel to every American. We have promised that we will give the gospel to every person on the earth by the year 2000. We have done this in spite of the odds that are against us, the opposition of some religious groups, the evident impossibility of doing it, the obvious inadequacy of our resources and purpose. In spite of all this, we say: *in this generation we will tell the world about the Savior.*

This bold declaration says many things. First, it says we believe in God and that he is a rewarder of those who seek him. It says that we believe in helping needy and unbelieving men. It further says we are willing to be the bridge between God and man.

Why would anybody in the middle of a hostile society, where humanism reigns and naturalism subverts Christian faith, attempt such an impossibility as this in this kind of world? By all the standards of man, this is not the time.

We're doing it because we believe the Bible, and this separates us from many others. The Scriptures unveil God. The Scriptures know and describe man. The Holy Book has a prescription for the disease of mankind. The Word of God is unique. There is nothing else like it in the world. All of the other holy books pale into insignificance when compared with the Holy Bible, the inspired Word of God. And this belief in

Scripture sets us apart from the unbelieving world. When we talk about *mankind,* we don't sound like unbelievers. We don't think about people like they think. Hopefully, we don't act like they act. We don't misunderstand love like they do. The Book separates the people of God.

Naturalism claims that the world just happened. It says that what we see with all of its complexity, magnificence, beauty, and purpose is simply the result of the "fortuitous concourse of atoms." The Bible says, "In the beginning God created the heavens and the earth" (Gen. 1:1, KJV).

The world states that man is a higher order of animal; he is the result of the evolutionary process. He is no more or less than a bundle of activated chemicals that has a certain level of superiority over the rest of the mammals on the earth, and when he dies, that's it.

The Bible says, "God created man in his own image, . . . male and female created he them" (Gen. 1:27, KJV). This undoubtedly means, among many things, that he created us with a capacity to know him and to reason and to anticipate; and an ability to have fellowship with God.

This creative act of God means that we are not mindless robots being controlled by the push buttons of environment. We are the creatures of God, and every one of us has the potential for being a child of God. No wonder one of the philosophers cried, "Leave *now* to dogs and apes; man has *forever.*" "Created in the image of God" certainly means that we are responsible to God for ourselves. Determinism parrots that man is not responsible for his plight and can do nothing about it. The Scriptures affirm that under God something can be done.

Naturalism spouts that there is no such thing as ultimate reality; there is nothing beyond that which we see, touch, taste, and feel. The Bible says there is ultimate reality in the fact that God is, that he reaches out to man, that man can transcend the rest of the created order, and that man can participate in ultimate reality through his partnership with God in His purpose on earth.

The mass of people believe there is no such thing as eternal accountability and responsibility. The Bible says, "It is appointed unto men once to die, but after this the judgment" (Heb. 9:27, KJV). The world says the answers are to be found in things—in money, possessions, houses, cars, boats, land. This is "where it's at." The Bible says, "Man shall not live by bread alone, but by every word that proceedeth out of the mouth of God" (Matt. 4:4, KJV). The Bible says that a man's life does not consist in the abundance of the things which he possesses—"Seek ye first the kingdom of God, and his righteousness; and all these things shall be added unto you" (Matt. 6:33, KJV).

The world says that you're alone, that you're a victim, that you're helpless, and there isn't anything you can do about all your troubles. Christ says, "Behold, I stand at the door, and knock:

if any man hear my voice, and open the door, I will come in to him and will sup with him, and he with me" (Rev. 3:20, KJV).

The world says that you die and that's all. The Book assures us that the Lord said, "I will come again, and receive you unto myself; that where I am, there ye may be also" (John 14:3, KJV).

What stark contrasts! The Scripture and society! We have a choice—the world and its fantasies, its hopelessness and emptiness—or the Book and its reality.

As Baptists we emphasize the Book because it is the gospel that is the "power of God unto salvation to every one that believeth." It is the Book that lays upon us, who rejoice in the bounties of God, the enormous responsibility for sharing the message. There is placed on us no ultimate responsibility for the propagation of the joys of the humanities, but there is a mandate from God that we share the truth of his Word. In our time the need has never been more evident and the opportunities more inviting.

The exposition of the Word of God is a mandate to Southern Baptists, and we must pursue it in whatever fashion we're capable of, wherever we are, under whatever circumstances we live, in whatever places we can go, with whatever power God will lend us for the task.

The study of the Word of God must go on in our churches in the Sunday Schools. The Sunday School is still the best evangelistic agency of the church. What better plan can be devised than to have an interested Sunday School teacher who studies the Word of God and shares it on the Lord's Day with those who gather? If somehow we can get these folk who are lost, those whose lives are filled with misery, who dabble in the deceits of the world, into the Bible-teaching program of the church and make certain that it is the Bible that is taught and not yesterday's ball game, we have an enormous advantage.

How remarkable it is when the Sunday School gets an unbeliever involved in the Word of God, with a warmhearted friend or teacher praying for that person that they may come to understand the truth of the gospel and have faith in Christ! The warmth of the small-group fellowship, the support that comes to the individual in those circumstances, the certainty that here is someone who loves and cares—we could not duplicate this kind of ready-made situation for the propagation of the gospel. It is in this kind of setting that the priests of God, our so-called lay people, most effectively multiply the ministry of the Word.

In my judgment there needs to be a revival of the exposition of the Word of God from the pulpit. It is not enough to claim orthodoxy and brag on the Word of God and give one's opinions to the folk on Sunday. What they need is the meat of the Word, under the influence and power of the Holy Spirit. This is God's way, and we claim it for our own. It is the emphasis on the truth of the Scriptures that has made us.

If we continue, this emphasis will sustain us.

Who is to do all of this? The Book says, "Christ loved the church and gave himself for it" (Eph. 5:25, KJV). It is the church and the people who are to take up the sword which is the Book. The church is the "thing." The instrument of God in doing his work is not the denomination or its agencies. The instrument God chose is the church. He has called the church the bride of Christ, the body of Christ, the people of God. This means that the church—your church, my church—bears ultimate responsibility for the propagation of the gospel.

Let's look for a minute at your church, the one where you go Lord's Day after Lord's Day and mid-week after mid-week. Think back to the emphases of your church last year. How much confrontation was there of the gross evil in your community, on television, in the motion pictures, in the clubs, and the society of which you are a part? How often was evil challenged? How much information was there given in your church last year about the judgment of God on sin? How many sermons were preached on the individual's responsibility for himself before God? How much emphasis was put on conviction for sin? How many times was the gem of repentance held up for the people to see, experience, and enjoy in new cleansing?

How much talk was there about the new life in Christ, a life that is different from that of the world? A life that makes serious demands upon individuals, a life that requires obedience and a clean walk? How many sessions were there in teaching people personal evangelism? How many disciples did you win last year? How many people did your church baptize?

Yes, the command of the Book belongs to the church, "Ye shall be witnesses unto me" (Acts 1:8, KJV). This is a call to relate to persons—to get the gospel to individuals. One of the practical problems that we face in our time is the intimidation of the multitudes. How on earth can such a small struggling group meet the needs of so many? Across the years, it becomes crystal clear that we probably could never confront the millions, but we can go to the man across the back fence, to the children who live next door, and to the lonely old folks across the street. As the church scatters through the city during the week, scores of opportunities are provided to us all.

I'm so glad that God did not call us to win the world, but that he called us to be witnesses. Your church (you) witnesses to the people where you live, to the folk you know at work, to the people whose lives you can influence.

A second aspect of this command of the Book to the church is that we shall "teach them to observe all things whatsoever he hath commanded us." Yet we seem to have raised a generation of Baptists who do not know what they believe. We suffer from the inroads of the parachurch movement and influences. We lose churches to the so-called "independents."

Our people pour millions into the pockets of those who make charismatic appeals by radio and television and who are never required to give a financial accounting to anyone. We ought to tell our people never to make a contribution to a cause that will not furnish them a financial statement. No money should be given to institutions that are owned by individuals instead of churches or denominations. We have such problems largely because our people do not know who they are or what we are.

I know of no shortcut to developing disciples. It has never been easy, but the truth of the matter still stands: doctrinal stability depends on lay people who know what they believe. In our time, with the inroads of the cults with appealing leaders making private pitches for their own welfare, great confusion reigns among many of our people about the truth of God, about what really is important, about their own values, and about what God's Word says.

One of Satan's principal battlegrounds is the place where he fuzzes up theological truth, where he gets us to fighting about the wrong things, where he blurs the lines of belief, and where he teaches our people that, after all, "it doesn't make much difference what you believe as long as you're sincere." If Bold Mission is to succeed in our time, there must be a new birth of helping people to develop in the likeness of Christ, "teaching them to observe all things whatsoever

I have commanded you" (Matt. 28:20, KJV). This entire concept is alien to the society. It will make us uncomfortable with our peers!

If we are going to achieve this monumental goal, the church must make every Christian a full partner. The priesthood of the believer is more than a noble idea—it is the basis on which we must build the proclamation of the truth. This means that the evangelistic task does not belong to the pastor, the church staff, or the deacons. It belongs to *every Christian.* Our polity demands this approach, the Bible teaches this approach, the world needs this kind of an effort. There are not enough paid ministers in all of the world to touch a fraction of the need in our day, but there are enough Christians who believe his Book to do what he wants done *if* we enlist every one of them in the cause.

One of the aspects of our obedience to the divine command must involve our money. Never in the history of the faith has it been so possible for an ordinary Christian, located in a church in the middle of the plains or high in the mountains, to participate in a world-mission effort. Every child of God can live dramatically through his giving and can participate in everything that God is doing through the world's largest evangelical mission force.

Every Baptist can participate in every social ministry, in every evangelism conference, in every new congregation the Home Mission Board leads in establishing through the Cooperative

Program. It is not enough to vote programs, or to say "amen" to theological orthodoxy, or to vow to do better in the future. Our life-style today makes it possible to contribute as much as we can spare to the cause of Christ in one or more of the efforts that we're undertaking.

Bold Mission Thrust. A slogan or a consuming passion?

It is not an easy decision: do we go along with the culture or do we plan confrontation in the name of Christ?

3
Dangerous Bold Dream

Reshaping a world in turmoil and reorienting a people in panic seem staggering, even impossible tasks. Yet, with the Word of God as a foundation and with a dream as bold as the Holy Spirit can conceive, the dimensions of the potential response correlate with the gigantic size of the task.

Our bold dream is solidly centered in the gospel. The summary in 2 Corinthians 5:19-21 is particularly appropriate here:

"God was in Christ, reconciling the world unto himself, not imputing their trespasses unto them; and hath committed unto us the word of reconciliation.

"Now then we are ambassadors for Christ, as though God did beseech you by us: we pray you in Christ's stead, be ye reconciled to God.

"For he hath made him to be sin for us, who knew no sin; that we might be made the righteousness of God in him."

In our dream, we see Africa seething with nations just born and yet to be born, with the people constituting the largest "have-not" segment save Asia in the world today. We see people whose rising aspirations are bound to be defeated unless there is some sort of catastrophic intervention in the affairs of that continent. Look at Asia, its population multiplying at an astronomical rate, with billions of people who have never yet heard the name of Christ; who have never yet exercised the freedom of the ballot—many millions of whom have never yet had enough to eat on any one day in their whole lifetime. Out of the seething masses of people upon our earth in our lifetime we have seen nations rise and fall.

Germany and Japan are examples of nations that rose like rockets against the evening sky to bring horror and terror to the earth. They rose, and they were plunged into defeat. They rose again, with new societies, new emphases, new points of view, and new troubles.

Yet it is as though God is saying again as he said in Isaiah: "The nations of the earth are like a drop from a bucket" (40:15, RSV). They are to him as a very little thing. And in this mass of people, in this rise and fall of the nations, one can almost trace historian Arnold Toynbee's thought—even in our own nation—that if a civilization rises to meet the demands and challenges of its day, it continues. If it does not rise to meet the challenge, it wanes, and God raises up another.

In any event, we should agree that the hand of God has been on our own nation in a manner unparalleled in the history of mankind. Nobody ever before us in the history of the earth has had so much. Never have so many "common people" been possessed of so many of the earth's goods. No nation ever before has had the might and power that this nation presently has. No nation ever before has had all of the freedom, with the resources to exploit it, which is enjoyed with such unlimited abandon by its people.

Ours is a nation possessing all of the institutions necessary for the promulgation of knowledge—even of truth. It is backed by all of the resources that are necessary for keeping its place as the leader of the free world—yes, even the entire world. It is backed by all of the know-how necessary, at least from a human view, to sustain its position. God surely must have thrust the United States on the face of the earth for such an hour as this. Nobody—no nation—has ever been in such a situation.

Since we are thrust into this position, we are immediately confronted with the challenge of the rest of the world with its infinite need, with its unlimited sin, with its vast corruption, with its lives lived on the very periphery of civilization. No one has ever had so much before, and nobody ever faced such an opportunity as you and I have in this hour. No one has ever faced the responsibility which we bear in such a unique way. This is not to criticize others. It is simply self-analysis.

There are those in Christendom who believe

that this is the post-denominational era—that the great denominations which rose in the seventeenth and eighteenth centuries in our country are now rapidly disintegrating. Many leaders in some of the so-called mainline denominations in our country have the feeling that their day has come and gone, and now they face a new era of declining denominationalism and ebbing strength. One of the leading religious publishers in this country told me not long ago, "If my denomination does not come back to the biblical base with the old-fashioned teaching of Christian evangelism, there is no hope for us." In this post-denominational era, Southern Baptists stand alone as the single old-line major denomination that is still growing. Our growth may be marginal at best.

Yet, denominational agencies, churches, individuals—all kinds of groupings of people—are responding to this dangerous bold dream. Louis R. Cobbs, secretary for missionary personnel of the SBC Foreign Mission Board, says he believes the Bold Mission emphasis is "beginning to be felt across the Convention in terms of appointment of people."

And he feels that the momentum will continue in 1979. "The number of inquiries, the interview schedules, the small-group meetings, the flow of correspondence, and the kinds of requests we're receiving, all indicate the level of interest is rising," Cobbs says.

Mission Support Division director R. Keith Parks of the FMB said, "It's my belief that Bold Mission Thrust is a small cloud on a distant horizon 'like a man's hand,' " referring to the Old Testament prophet Elijah's prayers for rain in ancient days (1 Kings 18:44).

"With the fervent praying of some modern-day Elijahs," Parks added, "I trust that its full force will be thrust out to a lost world in our day."

First Baptist Church of North Augusta, South Carolina, has planned to provide personnel for building an assembly in Tanzania as part of its bold dream. This is believed to be the largest overseas volunteer project ever sponsored by a single Southern Baptist church.

The church is to send one long-term volunteer and around eighty short-term volunteers to the African country. By voting to accept the project, the church postponed construction of a new auditorium to accommodate the crowd which comes to two services each Sunday.

The construction is expected to cost around $135,000 and take two years to complete. It will serve Tanzanian Baptists in somewhat the same manner as many state assemblies are used by Baptists in state conventions in the US.

One church member, a construction firm office manager, is to serve in Tanzania as site engineer for the project. Other volunteers will go as their skills are needed. All of the volunteers are to have person-to-person ministries with the Tanzanians and will train them in construction and church-program skills.

A Foreign Mission Board spokesman says that the project "will have a ripple effect in voluntarism," and noted a 59 percent increase in one-year volunteers during 1978.

"Bold Going" is one of the three key concepts included in the SBC denominational emphasis for 1979–1982. The other two are "Bold Growing" and "Bold Giving." Related to Bold Going, career and short-term mission volunteer involvements are receiving major promotional support by the SBC mission agencies.

One specific goal for the time period is to encourage churches to seek out the called, and to cooperate in supporting five thousand Mission Service Corps personnel, as well as other short-term mission volunteers.

"The Lord really knew what he was doing when he sent Ed Mason to Ethiopia for a year as business manager," said Suzanne Gross, whose husband, Lynn, is treasurer of the Ethiopian Mission.

Ed and Vi Mason arrived in Ethiopia at a crucial time, serving for one year before all the Southern Baptist missionaries had to leave the country because of the war situation.

But during that year, Mason, an attorney from Tallahassee, Florida, worked out a "management trust" agreement and filed it with the Ethiopian courts to allow Baptist mission work to continue in Ethiopia even after the missionaries had to leave.

Gross said he and his wife were convinced that God sent them a lawyer as business manager to work out the complicated legal document.

A partner in a law firm, Mason had held public office several times in the state of Florida, including terms as a judge, as county commissioner of Dade County, and as Tallahassee's public service commissioner.

Even though it wasn't really time for him to retire, when Mason discovered he could combine overseas travel with service for the Lord, he retired early.

"This has been one of the greatest blessings of my whole life. It's wonderful to work with such people who are so uniquely qualified to do what they're doing. I've never been associated with people who have such a rich spiritual dedication. They have the assurance that God is leading."

And so a bold dangerous dream can become a reality.

In Houston, Texas, the dangerous bold dream has so gripped Sagemont Baptist Church that members have decided to double all mission giving and increase personal missions efforts in 1979.

The increased giving did not automatically happen. It stems from the fact that the church and many of its members have become debt-free, according to pastor John Morgan and minister of missions Hal Boone, a paraplegic who formerly served as a missionary physician in Africa.

The 2,500-member congregation gave $55,000 for worldwide missions through the SBC's Cooperative Program in 1978, a substantial increase over 1977's total of $46,200. But it has voted to double Cooperative Program gifts to $110,000 in 1979.

To further support Bold Mission Thrust, the church will also double its special mission offerings and its monthly gifts to the Union Baptist Association.

Sagemont decided to become debt-free when Morgan realized that churches of the Union Association paid more interest on loans than was given for missions. The church's debt-free status resulted from Financial Freedom Seminars Morgan developed a few years ago. About two hundred couples are similarly debt-free.

As a church, declares Boone, "we are never planning to borrow any more money. We're going to build a new building and pay cash for it."

The pastor decided that the church should employ a missions minister rather than a minister of recreation, a position which had been under consideration. He felt that the latter need could be handled by a part-time person.

Boone, a former medical missionary in Tanzania, Uganda, and Kenya, leads the Sagemont church in begining a worldwide mission program even though he is a paraplegic. While in Kenya, where he was a physician and famine relief administrator, Boone's car rolled over, fracturing eight of his ribs and injuring his spinal cord.

"If I had those past twenty years (in the mission field) to do over again, I'd do it all over again," he said. "It's been a wonderful experience. We felt divine leadership in it. If the opportunity ever comes, we'll go again—if the opportunity comes for a guy in a wheelchair to serve."

Boone says the increased church budget will help Sagemont support volunteers through Texas Baptists' Rio Grande River Ministry, the Home Mission Board, the Foreign Mission Board, and the SBC Mission Service Corps.

"We already have a 22-year-old woman who has turned in her application for work in Brazil with students," Boone said. "What's happening at the church is a miracle."

A miraculous response to a dangerous bold dream.

One measure of the way Bold Mission Thrust has captured and stirred the imagination and creativity of a denomination is the unprecedented interest and involvement of the President of the United States.

Amid denominational planning for Bold Mission, President Carter asked several Southern Baptists to lunch at the White House. The heads of the Home Mission Board, Foreign Mission Board, Sunday School Board, representatives of the Woman's Missionary Union and Brotherhood Commission, and a few others were there.

The luncheon took place in the Roosevelt Room of the White House, with portraits of Teddy and Franklin looking down at the group. At the appointed hour, the president was in the room. He came around the circle of guests, greeting each one. He chatted, telling interesting family anecdotes, and shortly invited us to be seated. "I want you to have your soup, and then there are some things I want to say to you," he said. He asked layman Owen Cooper, a former president of the Convention, to ask the blessing, just as one would in his own home.

We began our meal with bean soup. After President Carter had taken a few spoonfuls, he began to talk and we listened. We soon realized that one doesn't eat bean soup while the president of the United States is talking!

He began with Baptist statistics. Without notes—for he had done his homework—he remarked that there are thirteen million "of us" and thirty-five thousand Southern Baptist churches. About five thousand missionaries, home and foreign. And he said that we're doing more than anybody else is doing, but we aren't doing very much.

If we were doing as well proportionately, he noted, as the Latter-Day Saints, who now have twenty-six thousand of their young people scattered over the earth, we would be saturating the earth with Baptist missionaries.

He commented that he was joining us late in denominational leadership and apologized for it. But he was joining us all the same. He thought it would be presumptuous for him to tell us, who lead the denomination, what this was all about. But there was something on his heart he must share with us.

He told us about his mother who went to India as a Peace Corps volunteer after she was seventy. She learned an Indian dialect in three months. At the end of that three months they changed her assignment and she had to learn another one. But in six months she knew two Indian dialects.

He suggested that what Southern Baptists ought to do is to ask every able widow in the Southern Baptist Convention who has enough money to live on to go as a missionary somewhere; and every student who has not yet gotten life together, who could be supported by his or her family or church, could be asked to go someplace as a missionary; and every retired couple, with enough money to live on, who feel that they want to do something worthwhile—ask them to hold a hand in Harlem or Hong Kong and tell those folks how much they are loved, and how Christ died for them.

He thought we should get every competent person in the Southern Baptist Convention, who has any kind of means of support, and double what we have now in the next five years, and quadruple the number of missionaries we send by the year 2000.

The president said we need to have a very short training period, a very intensive orientation period, and then send them; let them do what they can do in the name of Jesus Christ.

It boggles the mind to hear the president of the United States talk in terms of sending people as missionaries to the lost. I could not, with my pragmatic orientation, help but say to him: "But Mr. President, the political implications of this could be devastating for you!"

He replied that I should not worry about the political implications. He understood them and would take care of them. He suggested that I forget it.

And when we had visited awhile and exchanged opinions back and forth, the time for the president's appointment with the ambassador to the United Nations came. He smiled at us with that great big Carter smile, and looked at us with those steel-blue eyes. "If you don't do something about it," he challenged, "I will."

It was obvious that such a challenge delivered by such a man was not to be taken lightly, nor was the accompanying offer: "Ask me to do anything I can do, and I will do it."

Before the afternoon was over, the group decided on some things we wanted him to do. We called the White House to say, "Mr. President, would you make a color videotape for us to present at the Southern Baptist Convention? We would like you to tell them what you've said to us."

In two days, the tape was ready, and it was shown at the Southern Baptist Convention where it had an enormous impact. The Convention voted overwhelmingly to back an effort to double the number of missionaries in the field by 1982.

What an impossible dream! Suppose we failed? What psychological, financial, and denominational problems would result? How would this effort affect our relationships with other Christian groups, with other governments, and the like? This is a dangerous undertaking.

A dangerous bold dream, rapidly becoming reality.

4
The Church the World Needs

When we acknowledge that people are in panic and our world is in turmoil—and when we agree that spiritual answers are the key to unlocking solutions to these problems—we are faced with the necessity of describing a response in terms of the church the world needs.

The church. *Your* church. The church you regularly attend—where you worship, engage in Bible study, and other activities and ministries. You may be significantly involved with your church, or you may hardly know the pastor's name. As we discuss the church, we consider the church I believe God would want us to have, the local congregation of believers, gathered—and dispersed—to achieve his work.

We are thinking here in terms of the New Testament church, the kind of model we discover in Acts:

"Then they that gladly received his word were baptized: and the same day there were added *unto them* about three thousand souls. And they continued stedfastly in the apostles' doctrine and fellowship, and in breaking of bread, and in prayers.

"And fear came upon every soul: and many wonders and signs were done by the apostles. And all that believed were together, and had all things common; And sold their possessions and goods, and parted them to all men, as every man had need.

"And they, continuing daily with one accord in the temple, and breaking bread from house to house, did eat their meat with gladness and singleness of heart, praising God and having favour with all the people. And the Lord added to the church daily such as should be saved" (Acts 2:41-47).

I have been very interested, as I have grown a little older, in trying to define what it is that Baptists mean when they say, "New Testament Church." It is absolutely astonishing to consider what we blame on God and sometimes what we claim to find in the New Testament.

We usually measure the function and the nature of the church by whether or not it is orthodox—orthodox according to *my* standards, orthodox according to *my* judgment, orthodox according to the way *I* see things, the way *I* understand eschatology, and all the rest. But you seldom hear a Baptist church measured by any standard other than its doctrine, its orthodoxy, or its statistics.

And yet, when you begin to study the New Testament, you find an enormous number of qualities, good and bad, that were found in the congregations of believers in the time that God was leading in the writing of the Scriptures.

I suggest that the church we need today is one which strives for the New Testament pattern, and I want to begin with its theology. *The theology of the church today, as always, is crucial to its function.* We spend more time arguing about orthodoxy than we do practicing it. All the same, it is infinitely important what we believe. It is infinitely important what the church practices, so far as its doctrine is concerned.

We have today, in my judgment, a creeping kind of universalism that has been made respectable by higher education, and naturalism, which is the accepted philosophy of our time and often confused with science. This creeping universalism is not taught in our theological seminaries. I repeat, it is not taught in our theological seminaries. It is a creeping kind of universalism reflected by our society. Our societal structures—and our appreciation of each other, and our unwillingness to draw lines and make divisions—tell us that people without Christ really aren't as bad as we in the past have made them out to be. What they really need, some seem to believe, is acculturation that will make them acceptable in our congregation of affluent and well-mannered people.

If a society, as ours does, continuously tries

to avoid accountability for its conduct, tries to place the blame on somebody else, tries to shift the responsibility to other shoulders, it is almost inevitable that the church will take on something of the color of the society in which it lives. Thus we have multitudes of people who believe that there is no final accountability to God for what we are. The society may avoid accountability, but God requires accountability. And if the church does not believe that men and women are lost, without hope in this world and the world to come, without Jesus Christ, there is no place for evangelism, and there is no theology of missions.

We might just as well face up to the hard facts: Are we willing for people in this educated, affluent society to laugh at us and say, "These crazy Baptists believe in hell fire and damnation, and they believe that people are lost without Christ and are without hope!"?

Can we face up to the acceptance of what the world says about folk who believe such narrow theology? The truth of the matter is, multitudes of people are not very concerned about those away from the church and away from Christ because they do not really believe that they are eternally lost. It is a tragedy for that to occur in our kind of world and in our time upon it, and yet I am convinced that there are hosts of educated or acculturated Southern Baptists who aren't genuinely concerned about unsaved people, because somehow we have grown comfortable in the shifting of accountability, and some believe that "if they're sincere and nice, everything is going to be all right."

The theology of the New Testament is crucial to the success of the church. *Its Lord is central to its nature.*

We say we believe in the lordship of Christ. But I would like to ask you to do a little exercise.

How many Baptist churches do you know, about which you can honestly say, "I believe the Lord Jesus Christ is running that church"? The question is embarrassing, isn't it? It's embarrassing because there are so many evidences that he isn't in charge at all. And the test of whether the Lord is the Lord of your church is the active work of the Holy Spirit in the church. The test is whether the Holy Spirit is convicting people—saved and sinners alike—of sin. "And He, when He comes, will convict the world concerning sin, and righteousness, and judgment," the Lord says as recorded in John 16:8 (NASB).

How long has it been since you have seen someone so convicted of their evil and wrongdoing that they are shattered in the presence of the holiness of God? How long has it been since you saw someone prostrate on the ground or floor begging for God's forgiveness of their sins. How long?

The test of the lordship of Christ is the work of the Spirit of God in the church, convicting those of sin, cleansing the lives of Christians, directing the affairs of the individual congregation, empowering the ministry on Lord's Day morning of the Sunday School teachers, of those who are personal witnesses. The evidence of a moving, surging power of Christ in the church is an accurate test of the lordship of Christ in your church.

And if these are not going on in your church, and you are saying, "We believe that Jesus Christ is the Lord of the church," perhaps you should discover who is running the show. Too many times for our comfort somebody else is running it besides the Lord Jesus Christ. But if Jesus is running it, the evidence is the response to the work of the Holy Spirit in the life of the congregation. If that's going on, Jesus is there. And if those evidences of his presence are not present, he isn't running the church, whatever else may be going on there.

In the New Testament church we need so desperately, *worship is basic to its mission.* So many times we say that we go to church to worship. But I must admit that sometimes I go to church and sit there while the pastor is preaching what usually is a splendid sermon, and I'm solving my personal and professional problems, and that's not worship. That's not worship, as worthy as it may be. Sometimes I'm thinking about where I have to be the next week, and constructing a sermon that I'm supposed to preach. Now I recognize that I'm perhaps more evil than you who read this, but the question that needs an answer is, "Do *you* worship when you go to the church services?"

When you sing a magnificent gospel song like "Glorious Is Thy Name, O Lord," do you sing it and mean it? What a great and wonderful name He has. Or do you put the phonograph needle down on your mind and play the song through without having the foggiest notion of what it conveys? If you do, you do not worship, whatever else you do. You see, we have a tendency, because it is easier to do it, to play games about worshiping God. It is a lot easier to pretend than to really worship because it gets uncomfortable sometimes when you do worship.

Here's a worship experience:

"In the year that king Uzziah died I saw also the Lord sitting upon a throne, high and lifted up, and his train filled the temple. Above it stood the seraphims: each one had six wings; with twain he covered his face, and with twain he covered his feet, and with twain he did fly.

"And one cried unto another, and said, Holy, holy, holy, *is* the Lord of hosts: the whole earth *is* full of his glory.

"And the posts of the door moved at the voice of him that cried, and the house was filled with smoke" (Isa. 6:1-4).

Isaiah was in the presence of God! And he was overcome with the awesome, terrible, wonderful glory of it—a bewildering, mysterious, shattering experience—being face-to-face with God and in the presence of Deity.

"Then said I, Woe is me: for I am undone;

because I am a man of unclean lips, and I dwell in the midst of a people of unclean lips: for mine eyes have seen the King, the Lord of hosts" (Isa. 6:5).

When we come in contact with the eternal God, we do not feel like measuring our righteousness alongside somebody else's because we have seen the Lord. Whatever others are becomes inconsequential and unimportant, for God's perfect righteousness and holiness, God's judgment, God's infinite love make me see myself by the revelation of his Spirit as he sees me, and woe is me, for I am unclean. I am undone, and I dwell in the midst of a people who are unclean and undone. When we come into direct relationship to the Almighty God, it begins to positionize us in relationship to ourselves and to everyone else, and we don't worry about others' sins because we're confronted with our own.

Ah, but the glory of true worship! "Then flew one of the seraphims unto me, having a live coal in his hand, which he had taken with the tongs from off the altar: and he laid it upon my mouth, and said, Lo, this hath touched thy lips; and thine iniquity is taken away, and thy sin purged" (Isa. 6:6-7).

Now I don't know if we have become so sophisticated that the purging of our sin is of no significance, but when I think of God cleaning me up again, I would like to shout, "Glory! He cleaned me up!"

It is a constant need that we have, for the

tests and trials of life are frequent and demanding, and God must clean me out and clean me up over and over again. And worship occurs when we get in touch with him and see him for what he is; we see ourselves for what we are; then cry out in our sin; and he cleanses us from our sin.

Now this is the church at worship that we must have in our time. If we go marching out into the world telling people what great folk we are, or that all of them ought to be Southern Baptists, they're going to tell us to go fly a kite, or something less proper than that. They aren't interested in just being Southern Baptists. Their needs are too basic. Their problems are too manifold, and their loneliness is too great. They need what God can do. And if we have not communed afresh with him in order to hear his voice, feel his cleansing, and go out of that place exhilarated by his presence, then we're going to fail in the task of Bold Mission Thrust, for we shall be unequipped for what God is trying to do.

Isaiah saw God. He saw himself in his sins, he received cleansing, and in the adoration and thanksgiving of worship, he "also heard the voice of the Lord, saying, Whom shall I send, and who will go for us?" He then said: "Here am I; send me" (Isa. 6:8). Now that's the result of worship—getting our spiritual batteries recharged, getting ourselves in condition through the experience of God, his presence, his cleansing, and his power to go into a world that is hung up on a thousand things alien to the gospel of the Lord Jesus Christ and say, I know that cleansing is available for I have received it. I know that God is real for I have been with him today. I know that God can do something for you, because I have experienced the glory of God today. Wouldn't you like to know what God can do? And when the church goes out like that, people will listen. Its worship is basic to its mission, and *its fellowship establishes its credibility.*

Have you ever seen a revival during the middle of a church fracas? I have once or twice seen a revival end the church fracas, but I have never seen one in the middle of the church fuss. Either the revival doesn't start or the fracas is over, one or the other. Of course that doesn't mean that Baptists always ought to agree. It doesn't mean that we always ought to think alike, of course not. But it does mean *koinonía,* the fellowship believers in the likeness of Christ have with each other, is real and important. This is what God expects the church to have internally—a Godlike kind of love for each other, as well as love for God.

I almost never have seen a church fight that was about anything important. Nearly always it's about who's going to run the show. How many times has a church started, begun to move, and God brings in folk, and they are saved, and the church begins to grow. And the folks who have been in leadership are suddenly outdated, outgrown, and outmoded, and they don't think they fit anymore. Some of them do not want anybody new; they don't want any new leadership; they will have to give up theirs. They do not want any new power in the church; it will pass them by. They don't want any new leadership in the church because they know they can't occupy those posts. They don't want new people because if new ones come in, they won't be wheels anymore. Have you ever seen that? We need to remember that the fellowship of the church establishes its credibility in the world.

Jesus prayed to the Father in this magnificent passage, "That they all may be one; as thou, Father, art in me, and I in thee, that they also may be one in us: that the world may believe that thou hast sent me" (John 17:21). One of the reasons we have so much difficulty establishing our credibility in the world is because we don't act like we have been with Jesus at all.

Have you ever seen a great big, handsome brute of a boy marry a pretty little wisp of a girl and then spend the rest of his life trying to make her over? It works the other way, too. He married her for what she was and immediately tried to change it all. And she married him for what he was and immediately tried to change him, too. Baptist churches are like that. We sometimes try to make everybody look alike, think alike, talk alike, wish alike—*koinonia* has to do with acceptance, and the fellowship of the church validates its credibility in the world. If we can't get along with God's people, how do we expect to make an impact upon those who are not God's people? Its fellowship establishes its credibility.

In addition to the fact that the church must strive for the New Testament pattern, the *church must work at the New Testament purpose.* For a moment I would like to alter the order of the Great Commission of Christ to the church, and put first the part which says "teach them to observe all things whatsoever I have commanded you" (Matt. 28:20). The instruction of the church. We have had the tradition among Southern Baptists of winning multiplied thousands, yea millions, to faith in Christ. But we have had the tradition, also, of training a few dozen or a few hundred or a few thousand. But the "teaching them to observe all things" that he commanded is essentially as much a part of the commission of Christ to the church as that "ye shall go everywhere, teaching them and baptizing them, in the name of the Father and the Son and Holy Spirit."

The apostles' doctrine, by which the church lived and preached in those early days, had to do with what they were to be. It had to do with *how to do* and *what they were to do.* It had to do with the development of Christian character. It had to do with the nurturing of Christian character that would validate their teaching and their testimony. How to witness is a part of "teaching them to observe all things whatsoever I have commanded."

I think one of the great things going on in the Southern Baptist Convention right now is the cooperative effort between the evangelism section of the Home Mission Board and the Sunday School and the Church Training departments of the Sunday School Board. They are trying to formulate a pattern to help our people learn how to be witnesses and children of God in the community where they live. "Teach them to observe all things whatsoever I have commanded," and if in your congregation you've quit Church Training because you think it's smart to do so and unless you have substituted something better, you are omitting a very important part of the commission which Christ has given to the church.

One of the tragedies of our time is that we're raising a whole generation of Baptists who know little of what they believe; much of a whole generation of Baptists who do not know how to bear effective witness for Jesus Christ; many Baptists who do not know why they are Baptists, except they like the cut of the preacher's coat or the way he combs his hair or somebody was kind, or it was that congregation which led them to faith in Christ. "Teach them to observe all things."

The church needed to achieve a dangerous bold dream is a New Testament church—in pattern and in purpose.

The church, your church, in this time—what ought it to be? And what should it be doing? We shall deal with the rest of that purpose later.

5
The Only People God Has

We Baptists have a marvelous theological heritage about the call of God to persons in ministry. It is supported and has a corollary in our idea that every person is a priest before God. Unfortunately, our theology is better than our practice, and our statements are better than the actual carrying out of them day-by-day in our churches. "Called" is a word we often associate only with the ministry, with the mission force, or relative to some specific, segmented, isolated, and sharply defined function of ministry.

The word which we translate "called" is used scores of times in the New Testament, and it has many meanings. We are called, for example (as Paul wrote to the Romans), to salvation—all of us—the selected of God, the appointed of God, the separated of God, the brought-by-God to salvation. The word used in the text is the same we use for "called." Called to salvation. We Christians are all called, as Paul said to the Galatians, into grace, the grace of Jesus Christ; called out of separatism, legalism, and secularity into the grace of our Lord Jesus Christ.

He wrote to the Corinthians that we are called to peace. God claimed some for peace in Jesus Christ. He wrote to the Thessalonians that we are called into his kingdom and into his glory. Saturated with the love of God, the children of God were selected by God, separated by God, and called into the purposes of God. I believe it is a legitimate exegesis to note that all of these refer to all the saints of God, the Christians, the people whom God elected in Jesus Christ.

But Paul sometimes uses the word, and other words, in a little different sense. He said, for example, as he wrote to the Galatians in the first chapter, "God separated me from my mother's womb." And immediately there is resonance with the first chapter of Jeremiah's prophecy as you read that kind of language from the prophet.

Paul wrote again in Galatians 1, "I was called by his grace." Here are the same elements, the selection and the voice of God calling to grace that he used about the expression of all the Christians called to grace. He said, "God called me to reveal his Son in me." And I think other passages would allow that interpretation for all of us called by God to reveal his Son in us. But he declared more specifically and in an isolated and special sense, "He called me to reveal his Son in me that I might preach him among the heathen." And there is the deviation or separation from the broad stream of the call of God to all of the Christians, to some for specific kinds of service to do particular jobs in given situations.

Paul wrote to Timothy that he was not (not any of us are), but he especially, was not called according to his works. God did not select (either what we call the lay Christian or the professional church-related vocational Christian) us according to our works. Aren't you glad he didn't? None of us would have gotten in if he had called us according to our works. For our works were like Paul's works before his redemption, and Paul said in effect, "He didn't call me because I was good or because I had done right or because I lived righteously. He called me according to his own purpose of grace."

Now here one begins to wade in extraordinarily deep theological waters—"God called me according to the purpose of his own grace." This meant the actions of eternal Deity. This meant the separation, the sanctification, (to use the old-time expression that has adequate biblical base), the sanctification of the individual—basically the setting apart of the individual. God had a purpose in a person. God had a purpose in the church, but it goes beyond that. He had a purpose in individuals whom he would use for particular purposes. And he said "this calling," or perhaps he was saying more accurately, "this grace." I rather think it was the grace which was given us in Christ Jesus before the world began.

There is terrible confusion in today's theology about the person of the Lord Jesus Christ, but

Paul is speaking of the pre-existent Christ. The eternal God had in his mind grace from the foundation of the earth. He, in that grace, is working out his purpose to bring together believers in Christ, that they in turn may become the instruments of God in reaching out to the rest of the world. Why? So that God's grace may be repetitive in its effect, and that the cycle of salvation, purification, equipping, calling, and commissioning the called would again repeat itself again and again.

As Paul spelled out the facets of his own call, he said, "I am appointed"—the sovereign act of God. This boggles the mind—that the eternal God would deal with us. We believe the eternal God specifically puts his hand upon individuals and says, "I want you, all of you, all of you all the time. All of you, all the time, with everything you are, with everything you can become, with everything you can accomplish." And Paul said, "God appointed me a preacher." A "herald" perhaps is a better translation of the specific word which he uses, and he uses here the word that has to do with the marvelous message of God's grace. "I am the herald, the proclaimer, the preacher of God's marvelous message of grace."

He went a little farther. He said, "I am also an apostle." The apostle was one who personally had been with Jesus Christ, and the apostle was also one *sent forth* by the Christ. And Paul said, "He was seen of me also, as of one born out of due time." He saw Him, however, and He brought Paul to his knees and to his senses and to his sight, and then He sent him. Paul said, "I am an apostle," or in effect, I am a preacher, I am a teacher, and I have a special assignment, an assignment to the Gentiles. He, in other places and in other translations, calls it an assignment or a special assignment to preach to the heathen. With that as a backdrop, let us put before us the call of God to some others and to ourselves, the wonder of the call of God to people.

Jeremiah is recorded as saying in chapter one of his prophecy, "Before I was conceived . . ." —God said to him, "Before you were conceived, I knew you. Before you were born, I sanctified you (I set you apart), I separated you." God made for himself a man! "Before you were conceived I knew you and before you were born I separated you." We can assume God had specific objectives for the total energy and life, for all of the mentality and personality of this man. Uniquely and personally Jeremiah belonged to God.

Without doing violence to the text, without attributing to us who have been called to special kinds of vocational service that which is not there, I think we can assume that God knew us and planned us. He may very well have said in the councils of eternity, "There must be a person like this with these qualities, with these elements of surrender, with these mental capacities, with these personality potentials. Here are some people who must fulfill the functions to which I shall call them throughout their entire ministry." He knew us, and he planned for us to participate in what he was doing in the earth— both those who are called to vocational service and all of those Christians, who are called into his grace and into the ministry of the fellowship of the gospel.

Now when God looked at Paul, he must have been enormously satisfied, particularly at the end of the apostle's ministry. When God looked at Jeremiah, he must have been happy, especially with certain segments of Jeremiah's ministry when he suffered untold difficulty and hardships in carrying out the purpose of God. What do you suppose God thinks as he looks at us?

One of the cartoons that sticks in my memory is of a mother and a father looking at a 1965-style son with dirty, sloppy clothes, a guitar hanging around his neck, with dirty hair way down his back (hair that hadn't been washed in a long time), with his beard all tangled, a cigarette drooping out of the corner of his mouth. The caption reads: "To think we planned that!"

I wonder sometimes when God looks at us what he thinks. How far have we strayed from his call? How far away from his purpose is the impetus of our lives? How far from the total surrender of personality and self? How far away from the exercise of the total mentality with which he endowed us? How far away from the yielding of all of our personality to his purpose? What does God think when he sees us? But he wanted us, he called some of us to special service, and all of us to the gospel servanthood in the sense of the proclamation of the faith. He wanted us. He wanted us for his own. He wanted to use us, and he set in force all the motions to save us and to call us.

Have you ever gone back in your mind and tried to think through all of the things necessary for God to do for your redemption? In my own case, I think about my country preacher father. I think about a godly mother with a will of iron. I think about the circumstances of the little church where I grew up. I think about the influence of Sunday School teachers. I think about the prayers of my mother and my father. And to this day, though they've long been in glory, one of the great memories of my life has been remembering my parents calling my name around the supper table. We didn't have dinner. We had that at noon. Around the supper table at night, they called my name before the throne of grace. All the things that God did to bring us to redemption, all the things he did to call us to become a part of the church of Christ, all the things he did to set in motion the mechanism that would make us his saints and thus his servants! The essential in that act was that he would sanctify us, separate us, set us apart for his service.

Look for a minute at the nature of his call— not, as Paul said, because of our goodness. We are all called first to salvation, as he said to Timothy, to the total surrender—all of us to the total surrender in a relationship to Jesus Christ. What a remarkable, startling, frightening thought— that we all have been called by the divine purpose of God to reveal Jesus Christ in us!

Not I, but Christ living in me, the visible Christ—the visible Christ in our lives. The visible Christ in the use of our mouths. The visible Christ in the way we think. The visible Christ in the utilization of our personalities. The visible Christ in the way we use our bodies. The visible Christ in our affections. The visible Christ in our ambitions. The visible Christ in our actions called all of us that he may reveal himself in us.

It is a holy calling. Paul said to Timothy, "this is a holy calling." A. T. Robertson translates that "a calling to a life of holiness." He called us to a life filled, saturated with, marked by, countenanced by, characterized by the holiness of the character of God. How far short of our calling as Christians, how far short of our calling as ministers of Christ do we fall from that calling to a life of perfect holiness? Paul, reiterating that call to be a preacher and a teacher, was saying that he was called to be an *understander* of God; called to be an expounder of God, an expounder of his grace.

There are then two great groups of "called" portrayed in the Scriptures. All of us as Christians are called to grace, peace, and witness; whoever makes the tragic mistake that the evangelistic and missionary task of the world is for preachers and missionaries only, misses the heart of the gospel idea related to our relationship to God through Jesus Christ. Some of us are designated for special duty (we would say vocational, full-time servants, missionaries, pastors, ministers—special areas of responsibility). All of us serve at his pleasure. He can change our place of service. He can differ our assignments from time to time. The essential nature of our response to the call, therefore, must be the response of total surrender to the purposes of God.

Additionally I think, from Jeremiah, Paul, and Christ, we can properly conclude that we are called to live dangerously. How much we may miss if we aren't careful in our time, for we are lovers of peace and so ought we to be. But we are also the lovers of tranquility which means the absence of conflict, and we may very well settle for tranquility instead of peace. We may be willing to settle for the absence of conflict when in fact, we ought to be willing to settle for the assault of the world upon ourselves and yet reside in perfect peace—in the peace that passeth understanding. You can be certain that if you are functioning under the call of God in the world in which you live, there are going to be attacks upon you and upon your ideas and upon your gospel, for Jesus taught us that we belong to him, and the world hated him and the world will hate us.

Does the adversary nature of a world that abhors the purity required of the gospel cause you to flinch and withdraw? Do you have enough

of the character of God in your life that the world
is assaulting you for your message and for the
purity of your living? He has not called us, either
the Christian in the church or the leader in a
place of special responsibility, to hedge us about
to keep us from suffering the defeats of the
world.

He has not called us always to be successful
according to the ideas of men, and this is a message that his churches need to learn. It may very
well be that, by the standards of the world, success will not attend the New Testament ministry.
By the standards of the New Testament, success
will attend it, but the success required by the
world and the success required by the New Testament are as far apart as east is from the west.
For if we are what we ought to be in the world
we will become a conscience to those who are
about us. We may function like the conscience
that causes a little boy to quit tearing up the
songbook when the preacher looks at him. Our
very presence in the place will be a condemnation of evil if we are essentially Christian and
are equipped for the work of ministry. He does
not hedge us about to exclude pain and defeat.

I'll tell you how he does hedge us about. He
hedges us about that we may be able to complete
the assigned task which he has given us. And
there's a vast difference between the peace of
God in one's heart and the absence of conflict
with a Godless society.

Now we've been thinking about two groups

of people. We've been thinking about two specialized kinds of functions in the proclamation of the gospel. One of these groups—the leaders, the pastors—has a specific responsibility to the rest. Paul said to the Ephesians that God has given some apostles and prophets and teachers, so the rest of the church—the people—may be equipped for the work of ministry. The pastor, the called of God, is the equipper of the people of God that they may do the work of God. And if he, the pastor/the leader, does not multiply his ministry through his people, he fails in what God expects him to do. It matters not how effective or how eloquent our orations may be, if they do not equip the people of Christ for the work of the ministry, we have miserably failed in the task of leadership that God has given us who have special calls.

But let me write a word about those whom we do not normally refer to as being the called, though surely they, according to the Scriptures, are called to grace, called to ministry, and called to proclamation.

The major task of Bold Mission Thrust belongs to what we call the laity of the church. If we're going to get Bold Mission Thrust done, it will be the whole church that does it. It's always the troops who bear the brunt of the fighting and not the officers of the corps. God works through all believers for many reasons.

He has them strategically deployed. Think for a minute about where all Southern Baptists live.

They're scattered from the ghetto to the far reaches of the mountains of the Rockies and the plains and the deserts and the countryside and the suburbs. God has people everywhere in America. Look how he has deployed the troops! Look where all the people live who are supposed to be bearing witness to the grace of Jesus Christ! Some people would call it life-style evangelism. God in his call for you to participate in proclamation has not put you where you are according to his purpose that you may enjoy it simply for yourself. He has put you where you are by way of strategically deploying the troops to do battle with evil and to carry the gospel wherever men stand in need. Each of these persons, every believer, has had an experience with the Lord. Each of these persons, every believer, is a priest before God, and should be representing man to God in intercessory prayer and in a unique and wonderful sense representing God to man—not interceders, not in-betweens, but all the same trying to bring the lost to the heavenly Father. The people of God called to grace and called to ministry—each of these persons has been gifted by God to do something in the kingdom enterprise.

In a New Testament church, there are all of the people with all of the gifts God wants in that congregation to accomplish everything God wants done there. Some who can teach; some who can witness; some who can sing; some who can wait on tables; some who can help with baptizing; some who can bear total witness; and all who can say, "This is what God has done for me, wouldn't you let him do the same kind of thing for you?" And corporately in that church— in every church that's following the purposes of God—there is available every type of service that is needed. God has supplied that need.

Years ago, when I was still a pastor, I had been talking about some of these things to our people, and we had been trying to get people to witness. We had been praying that God would call out of our church people equipped for the work of the ministry, and he was calling many young people for full-time vocational service in that unique call that God gives to some. But I think one of the greatest joys was that he was calling some with special gifts in personal witnessing. We were trying to do it using the Sunday School class as that reservoir of love and support.

One Sunday morning a young Sunday School teacher, I suppose in her thirties, came forward in the service. She accompanied a woman who was making a public profession of faith. She said to me, "Pastor, in our class we've been praying for this woman, and we've been witnessing to her. God has answered our prayers and here she is making a profession of faith." And I thanked her and talked with the woman, and it was genuine according to my ability to interpret. She united with the church and was baptized.

The next Sunday night, as I recall, the teacher came down the aisle with another woman, and she said to me, "Pastor, we've been praying for this woman and we've been witnessing to her. God has used this witness to lead her to faith in Jesus Christ," and again the repetition of the same experience.

The next Sunday she came and she said, "Pastor, I don't have anybody this Sunday, but would you pray with me about a woman?" and she called her name, and said, "We've done all we know to do and we've witnessed and we've prayed and we're trying to cultivate her. Will you pray for me and will you pray for her?" Routinely I agreed to pray, but I did remember to pray. The next Sunday or the Sunday after here she came with that woman by the hand, and she said, "God has answered our prayers." And when that profession of faith was made she said to me, "Now pastor, will you pray with me for somebody?" and called another name. I knew by now something unusual was going on.

One of the most remarkable experiences in my entire ministry was to see that woman come down that aisle Sunday morning and Sunday night, Sunday after Sunday after Sunday, either with somebody by the hand saying, "Pastor, she has made a profession of faith in Jesus Christ," or saying "Pastor, we can't seem to break through; we can't seem to get it done, will you pray with us?" I wish now, though perhaps it's good that I did not, that I had counted the number of times she said, "Pastor, will you pray with us?" for I came to believe that when that woman said, "We're praying for somebody," it would not be long until God did something wonderful.

There came a sad day when she said, "Pastor, we must leave the church, and we're going to a large city in Texas," and I knew we were losing a precious minister of Jesus Christ. Years later I went to a large church in that Texas city.

And I said to the pastor of that church, "Do you know her?"

"Oh yes," he said, "That's one of the most remarkable people I've ever known."

Two thousand people in Sunday School, but the preacher knew her. Sunday by Sunday she was still coming down the aisle saying, "Pastor, she's made a profession of faith—will you pray with us about somebody else?"

Called by God to the work of the ministry! *All of us.* Some of us in unique ways. But all of us called to grace and called to ministry.

What is the nature of God's call to you?

6
Bold Response

The beginning of planning for Bold Mission Thrust was reviewed for Southern Baptist agency leaders in the autumn of 1977 by Dr. Porter W. Routh, executive secretary-treasurer of the SBC Executive Committee.

Dr. Routh cited three Scripture passages which are at the heart of Bold Mission Thrust:

"The wicked flee when no man pursueth: but the righteous are as bold as a lion" (Prov. 28:1).

"Let us be bold then, and say, 'The Lord is my helper, I will not be afraid' " (Heb. 13:6, TEV).

". . . allow us, your servants, to speak your message with all boldness. . . . They were all filled with the Holy Spirit and began to proclaim God's message with boldness" (Acts 4:29,31, TEV).

God's Great Commission, Dr. Routh told the group, is a challenge to boldness. The church must be a miracle of boldness if it is to succeed. We have, he said, always been told to lengthen our cords and strengthen our stakes—to dream the impossible dream—to reach beyond our grasp.

During the Baptist Jubilee Advance, we were told of the boldness of Luther Rice and Adoniram Judson as they caught a vision of a lost world.

At the 1961 Southern Baptist Convention in St. Louis, the Executive Committee brought a recommendation that an advisory committee be set up which would represent the Convention agencies, the State Conventions, and the editors of state Baptist papers to look at alternatives and objectives, and then report to the Convention by 1963. This Post-'64 Advisory Committee brought its report in 1963, looking toward strengthening the church in worshiping, proclaiming, educating, and ministering in the 1965-68 period.

At the 1963 Southern Baptist Convention in Kansas City, emphasis was focused on "The Baptist Faith and Message." A year of "A Church Fulfilling Its Mission Through Evangelism and World Missions" was added to the emphases already planned for 1969, and a preliminary plan for planning was approved. A more detailed plan for planning was adopted by the SBC in Atlantic City (1964) for the period beyond 1969.

Meanwhile, in 1966, forty-one study groups involving 615 pastors and laymen had met in the "70 Onward" study. In these meetings, many individuals started talking about critical needs, and then concluded that bold actions would be needed to meet those needs. The convention's emphasis theme for 1969-73 talked about "Living the Spirit of Christ."

At the Southern Baptist Convention in Houston (1968), the messengers took a bold step by adopting "A Statement Concerning the Crisis on Our Nation" and started talking about more churches and more missionaries. Mrs. Marie Mathis of Woman's Missionary Union is reported to have started using the phrase "Bold Mission" about that time. It appeared in the 1970 SBC *Annual* with the themes for 1973-79, with the 1977-79 theme being "Sharing Christ in Bold Mission." By 1972, this had been changed to "Let the Church Reach Out." One way the church was to reach out was "by boldly confronting the secular world through bold mission."

At about the same time in 1972, preliminary meetings began for the denomination's "Impact 80" planning process. Feedback from across the country seemed to indicate a growing concern for Bold Mission. It is interesting to note that the Convention theme interpretation for 1977-79, which was presented to the denomination's Emphasis Coordinating Committee on January 19, 1971, said: "Churches should provide opportunities for dedicated youth and lay people to serve in short-term mission projects." It talked about "confronting all groups everywhere with the gospel."

Somehow, the Bold Mission idea, continues Dr. Routh, did not have much content until the Missions Challenge Committee reported to the

Convention at Norfolk in 1976 that Southern Baptists should set as their primary mission challenge "that every person in the world shall have the opportunity to hear the gospel of Christ in the next twenty-five years."

The SBC Stewardship Commission responded to the report by setting up a task force on "bold promotional plans" and presented to the Convention meeting in Kansas City (1977) a proposal asking the SBC Executive Committee to give "strong administrative leadership in promoting and coordinating all facets of Bold Mission, and adopt a single over-arching theme to promote the Convention's world mission goals."

The Executive Committee responded to the request. Dr. Routh assigned Dr. Albert McClellan as the coordinator. A plan was adopted by the Convention, and the theme of "Bold Mission Thrust" was adopted for the 1977-82 period.

There is in the first epistle of John, chapter 3, a remarkable passage that should support and strengthen all of us who belong to Him, and give us new insights, new strengths.

"Behold, what manner of love the Father hath bestowed upon us, that we should be called the sons of God: therefore the world knoweth us not, because it knew him not. Beloved, now we are the sons of God, and it doth not yet appear what we shall be: but we know that, when he shall appear, we shall be like him; for we shall see him as he is. And every man that hath this hope in him purifieth himself, even as he (Christ) is pure" (1 John 3:1-3).

Probably, never in the history of Southern Baptist life and perhaps never in the history of evangelical faith have so many talked so much about three words as much as Southern Baptists have in conjuction with Bold Mission Thrust in these last few years. Every denominational gathering, it seems, has majored on Bold Mission Thrust; has centered on the fact that God has commissioned us as Baptists, as Christians in the United States, to proclaim the gospel to every person in America by the year 2000 and to every person on the earth in the next generation. This is a mammoth phenomenon unknown in the history of evangelical faith. Nobody has ever quite gone at it like this before.

There have been more meetings than one can count. There have been more committees than one cares to remember. There have been more discussions than the mind of man can recall. More resolutions have been passed. More actions have been taken. More subcommittees have been appointed. More has been done about Bold Mission Thrust denominationally than just about anything in the history of the denomination.

Now all the talking (or much of it) has been done. All of the organizations are set. All of the mechanisms are in place. All of the denominational decisions have been taken. All of the denominational leadership has been committed. Everything has been done that leadership knows how to do. All the steps have been taken that seem necessary to get ready to do something magnificent for God.

And now the drum rolls are beginning to fade in the distance, and the hullabaloo is beginning to die out, and now the charge of enthusiastic electricity in the atmosphere is beginning to dissipate. All of the people who are needed are available. All of the resources that God needs are in the pockets of Southern Baptists. All of the organizations already exist. All of the institutions have been formulated. The theological seminaries are full of theological students. Everything is in readiness, and now it comes down to each individual.

Whether we get all of this done will not depend upon our theology. Billy Sunday used to say that some of the Christians he knew were as orthodox as the devil, and *nearly as mean.* Our orthodoxy is not seriously in question. Every once in a while, somebody rises up to say, "Southern Baptists are becoming liberal." If so, it's the only liberal denomination in the history of the faith that's trying to win the world to belief in Jesus Christ!

Our theology is not in question. We believe the Bible. We might argue about the words with which people want to describe it. We may not agree on the millennium, but I suspect none of us really know that much about it. We may argue about all kinds of interpretation, but the truth of it is, 99 percent of Southern Baptists believe that the Bible is the inspired Word of God. The problem is that a high percentage doesn't do very much about it. It is not the faith that is lacking; it is the work that is lacking. We have the faith.

No, the orthodoxy of Southern Baptists is not the problem in our time. The problem is the quality of persons—the quality of our own personhood. We need to ask ourselves, "Who am I? What am I? Why am I?"

For myself, I must begin with the fact that I am a child of God. What a glorious thought! When I was growing up in Mississippi, I was a "preacher's kid." When I walked down the street, I was the preacher's kid. When I threw a mudball at somebody, it was the preacher's kid who had no business engaging in such mischief.

When I was not the leader of the algebra class, it was the preacher's kid who should do better than that. When I *was* the leader of the algebra class, it was what was expected of the preacher's kid. It made no difference what I did, I was the preacher's kid. It makes no difference what *you* do, you are God's child. So let that begin your cognizance of it and your continued assimilation of it. That begins to bring into focus your entire experience—"I am God's child."

"I am God's child." We are not going to get far in Bold Mission Thrust until that comes home to us—that everything about us is surrounded by Him. We are hemmed in by him. We are corralled by his Spirit. We are dominated by his purpose. We are the children of God, and to act like anything else is gross evil in days like these. We are God's children, and our ambitions must be controlled by this concept. We are God's children, and our affections must be dominated by it. We are God's children, and our actions must be directed by it. We are the children of the King.

That begins immediately to establish us in relationships, in relationships to all kinds of folks, in the relationships that God desires his children to sustain toward one another. Who I am is not a community "big wheel" or social leader or prestigious pastor or wealthy first family or glamorous young matron or successful politician.

Who am I? I am God's child, and that is the supreme fact about my life. And as that supremacy begins to dominate who we are and what we are, and as we react to being his children, then our lives begin to "jell." We will never get anything done about all of those places where we need to be at work until there is the constant consciousness in our lives that we belong to God and he belongs to us, and we are inseparable. We are inexplicably bound up with what God is doing in the world. We are the children of God.

When I was that preacher's kid in Mississippi, everything that my father did reflected upon my life, and everything I did apparently reflected upon his reputation. But I was all bound up with being the preacher's kid.

I'll never forget the time in my childhood when a man sat with his automobile parked on the lawn of my father's house. All night long, my father and a friend sat with shotguns at the ready, for the man in the car outside had a sawed-off shotgun—and a .45 caliber pistol, waiting to kill my father's friend when he came out the front door. I was totally bound up in the ministry of my father.

I remember so well the time when the "town drunk" set his bunk on fire in the village jail and burned himself to death. My father was called out in the middle of the night that Saturday to tell a weeping widow that at last the inevitable had occurred. Her husband had finally destroyed himself. And I remember the sobs of his children as they finally let it penetrate their minds, though they fought to guard against it, that their father had died in jail. I was all bound up in that tragedy because it was the ministry of my father. And whatever he did, I was involved therein.

What a remarkable lesson for Southern Baptists to learn in such a time as this! We are bound up with all that our Father is involved in. We ought to be giving ourselves selflessly to what God is trying to do in the world.

We stand, some say, on the threshold of a great awakening. I have from time to time searched the history books to interpret the meaning of the Great Awakenings in this land. I have tried to determine in my own mind if this really furnishes a platform and a pattern for us to sweep across our land. What a thought, a wave of righteousness from sea to sea! Does it mean that God is about to quell the forces of evil in our midst? Does it mean that God is about to let us participate in bringing the soothing balm of redemption to America? Are we really on the threshold of a new spiritual awakening? If we are, God must have some people who are conscious of who they are—of their spiritual Father, of his labors upon the earth, of his proclamation as it is stipulated in his Word, of his Spirit as he works in our lives. We are the children of God.

The question is, are we going to act as though we are spiritual waifs, or are we going to join the family of Christ in the work of God where we are?

One of the pressing needs of our time is that we shall demonstrate to the world that we are the people of God in the world. He has said that we are to be in the world but not of it; we are to be living in the middle of it—just don't get infected by it! We are to give ourselves to it in service—just don't look and act like it. What a remarkable time it is when God calls us, as his children, to act like members of his family, with complete recognition of who we are and to whom we belong. How remarkable it is that he is calling us to give ourselves away in the purposes he is fostering!

Of course, that always brings up the question, not only "Who are you?" but "What are you?"

Well, I'm a born-again Christian. There seems to be a dual blessing and curse about the use of that phrase "born again" in our time. It is easier than ever to talk about being born again, but it is also a phrase that has been prostituted to mean much God never intended it to mean when he recorded it in John's Gospel.

What are you? We stand on the threshold of either holocaust or revival, and which it is will depend on the quality and the character of the people of God. What are you? What kind of individual is there behind the facade, behind the mask?

Some who live and work with the public for long years need to pull away and to feel aloneness and to seek a time of renewal and recuperation—a time when nobody knows who you are or why you are, when nobody calls your name or speaks to you. Admittedly, it is difficult to find circumstances like that, but some have done so. Some have even gone to an extreme—withdrawing from the battle of the Christian faith in our time.

By their very character, they have masked themselves before the world, and are not on the surface the people of God. These may be the sophisticates or the wealthy or the secure or the intellectual elites of our time. They may be the community leaders, the socialites of our era. They wear many masks, but they have ceased to be, in public, the people of God. What are you?

The Word tells us that man looks upon the

outward appearance but that God looks upon the heart. How do you view all those folks (who mill like ants in a hill) that you come in contact with day after monotonous day in your life? Do you see them as being ugly or pretty, wealthy or poor, bright or dumb? Or do you see them as persons for whom Jesus Christ died? You can learn a good deal about the quality of your religious experience as you analyze how you see individual persons. What do they look like to you? What are they worth to you? Are they important to you? What does God want you to do and to be toward other persons you encounter? How do you see persons?

Who are you? What are you? Why are you? What organizes your life? What are the built-in controls that make everything else subservient? What so dominates the nature of your living that it could well be said, "This is the *summum bonum* of my life? This is my all-in-all. This is my purpose for living. This is why I exist."

Your family should be involved in it. Your work is involved in it. But really, is not God asking Southern Baptists, "Why are you there at all? Why are you in the position you occupy? Why do you have the mind that you have? Why do you know all the people you know? *Why* are you, anyway?"

Our response needs to be along these lines: "I am because of the love of God. It is no longer I, but Christ who lives in me. Christ in me, the hope of glory. Christ in me, the means of control of my Adamic nature. Christ in me, that which drives me out of the bed when I am tired and that which sends me on another errand I feel I don't have the strength to do. Christ in me, making me love the unlovely, making me go when I would not, making me do more than I can. Christ in us, the hope of glory." *Why* are you, anyhow?

I shall not soon forget the last time I saw Leonard Sigle before he died. He had been before retirement superintendent of missions in Northern Nevada. There aren't many people in Northern Nevada, and many who are there seem to make their living from gambling and prostitution, though obviously not all of them do. Leonard had hands that were all gnarled and beat up. I used to think that each of his ten fingernails had been knocked off with a hammer at least three times. Leonard was not a sophisticated man. I don't know if he ever got his fingernails clean before he died. His face was seamed as though it had been exposed to the weather for fifty or sixty years, as indeed it had. And I suppose that when Leonard died, not many people knew about it. I finally found out about it weeks afterward, and I had a moment of private sorrow and private thanksgiving for Leonard Sigle.

You see, he had been out there in those mountains and hills of California and Nevada for thirty or forty years scratching out new little churches wherever God would lead him. And when I saw him, it was a love feast, because I loved, respected, and admired him. He and I were dear friends, though we rarely saw each other. When we could get through the crowds to one another and we had embraced, I took his rough hand in mine and said:

"Brother Leonard, how are you getting along?"

"Oh, Brother Grady," he said, smiling that great big crooked grin, "I'm off down there behind the mountain, and I'm building a church."

I have asked Leonard Sigle that same question about eight or ten times.

"Brother Leonard, what are you doing now?"

"Oh, I'm off down there behind the mountain," or "I'm off out there in the middle of a desert, building a church."

That last time I said to him, "Leonard, how many have you had a part in building now?"

He answered, "Aw, Brother Grady, God has been so good to me. This is number fifty-six."

Leonard Sigle knew *what he was* and *who he was* and *why.* He knew, and he gave it all away to the Father, who gave his only begotten Son.

7
The Bold Message

Have you ever stopped and asked yourself the question, "Do I really have anything to say to this crazy, mixed-up world we live in?" Do you have any message for my Hindu philosopher friend in Delhi? Do you have anything that would give him assurance first that there is no reincarnation, there is no endless cycle, and life is not determined by the stars? What would you tell my friend in Delhi?

What would you say to the hedonist who says, in essence, "Eat, drink, and be merry for tomorrow you're worm bait"? What would you say to the secularist who says "There is nothing to all this religious tommyrot; reality has to do with getting, keeping, enjoying, holding, knowing, and all the rest of these things"?

What is the message that we take to these people? That they should become Southern Baptists? I don't think so. I don't think so at all. People keep saying to us, "Do you believe only Southern Baptists are going to heaven?" No, I don't think some of us are going to make it. We're not trying to get them to be like us, for we're far too imperfect. We aren't actually trying to conform them to the image of the deep South, for some of us didn't come from there, and some of us know there are more important things. What do we have to say to these people?

We must, I believe, begin with the objective provision of God for the redemption of man. He looked upon us and he was moved with compassion, and he proposed before the foundation of the world to provide salvation. God invaded human history in the person of Jesus Christ— God incarnate in Christ Jesus of Nazareth who lived a perfect life, tempted in every fashion such as we are tempted, yet without sin. Crucified on a cross, and as Peter said, he bore our sins in his body on the tree. I don't understand all that that means, but I'm confident that it does mean he died in our place, he bore our sins, and he made possible our eternal redemption.

Further, on the third day God raised him up from the dead. There was no trick. There was infinite mystery. There was no confusion. God literally raised the dead up to life. He was seen by more than 500 according to Paul's testimony. His resurrection from the dead, Blackstone the great jurist used to say, is the most certain affirmation in all of human history. He said the laws of evidence are adequately fulfilled in the records of the resurrection of Jesus Christ from the dead.

After the time of Jesus' instruction of the disciples and the completion of God's work, he ascended back to the right hand of the Father. There, the Bible tells us, he intercedes on our behalf and promises us that he's coming again some day. I don't know how. I don't know when. I don't understand all the details. I'm not as bright as some people who contend they have it all figured out. I don't have that figured out, but he's coming again, and that's good enough for me!

The person who believes in Jesus Christ is reconciled unto God and has eternal life as God's free gift. This is God's objective provision for man's redemption, but all of this will not at first mean much to the people out there to whom we are witnessing. They are people who want to know, "What does all of this have to do with me? What does all of this have to do with the problems I'm having with my kids? What does all of this have to do with the tough time that I'm having at the office? What does all of this have to do with the fact that I am old and about to die? What does all of this have to do with me?"

We need to stop here and think about the three phases of salvation as we relate them to the persons we bear witness to. The nature of salvation, of course, begins with conviction for sin, with repentance for sin, and then by faith in Jesus Christ the new birth comes. "For by grace are ye saved through faith."

Now there was a time when I was happy that the words "new birth" were on the lips of the world. I'm not so happy about that anymore because the phrase has been twisted, warped, and confused, and now everything that has any kind of a change, according to the public press, has a "new birth." But Scripturally, the new birth means that a person in sin is given a right relationship to God in righteousness when he believes in Jesus Christ—not because of himself—for he has been made right with God because of the sacrifice of Christ and because he put his faith in Jesus. That's the Godward side of being born again. Being made in right relationship to God. Being given the righteousness of God through Jesus Christ. Being removed from condemnation. Or if you like the phrase better, "justification by faith" through the grace of the Lord Jesus Christ.

But one of the infinitely important things that we don't pay much attention to is: What happens to the person? What is the personward side of the experience of being born again or of being saved by grace through faith? Many things happen, but one of the things that happens is that the individual gets a new boss, a new master of his life. Self has been on the throne. Now Christ is Lord and self is dethroned, and deadly unbelief has given way to saving faith.

The person who has been in bad condition before God, now being born again by grace through faith, suddenly has something happen to him that makes him say, "What does God want from me? What is God's concern for my life? What is God's connection with my daily existence? How can I approach God and how can I relate to God?" He has a new master of his life when the Holy Spirit moves in and takes over. The Christ becomes alive in him. When the Spirit of God moves into our lives, we then in the new birth receive a new master.

Another thing that has eternal consequences happens when we're saved by grace through faith. It was best described by a preacher friend of mine many years ago. He was not a theologian. He and I were talking about theology one day. I'm not a theologian, either. We were discussing the problems related to the new birth, and so I said to him, "What do you think happens when a person is saved?" He scratched his thinning hair a minute, and he said, "I think the biggest thing that happens is that God changes his *wanter.*" God changes his wanter.

I think he hit a key element of Christian faith, for the newly born child of God wants different things. The unsaved person who is greedy goes on being greedy. While the newly saved man has residual elements of greediness, he doesn't like it in himself. He doesn't want that anymore. The unsaved person is filled with lust and goes on enjoying his lust, but the newly born child of God, though he may lust, abhors his lust. He doesn't want to be the kind of person he used to be. The person who is dishonest, unsaved, has no compunction about going on being dishonest, but the newly born child of God, though he may sometimes fall short and be dishonest, does not want to be dishonest—he wants to be honest. He wants to be right with God. He wants to be straight in his walk. He wants to be clean in his speech. He wants to be clean in his thoughts. He is not always, because he's still a person, a man or a woman, a boy or a girl, but his "wanter" has been changed.

There are those who have remarked to me, "When God saved me, he took away all desire to sin." Well, I just want to say that if that's what God always does, *I missed it.* He surely didn't take it all away from me.

I find, as Wordsworth once put it, "Our sins, they are with us waking; they are with us sleeping, and they rend us in our graves." I find in me many of the old evidences of my Adamic nature. I find in me constant temptation—maybe Satan has assigned all of his imps to me and he doesn't bother you, but he surely does work on me, night and day, day and night. But the person who has been born again, while he still falls into sin, has a new attitude toward it. Now he hates it.

One of the most interesting things that God does to us when we're saved is that he makes us miserable when we do wrong. You may slip into sin, but you're not going to enjoy it. God keeps probing away. He keeps working on your life. He keeps saying, "That is not proper for my child." So the new birth brings us a new attitude toward sin, and the Holy Spirit comes in and lives in us.

I doubt that there's as much confusion theologically about anything right now as there is about the doctrine of the Holy Spirit. But the Spirit of God, if I understand the Scriptures, comes to live in the newborn child of God. We do not always become immediately aware of that. We do not always submit to him. That does not alter the fact of his presence. We are not always ecstatic and on a high.

One of the worries I had about some Christians in the 1960s was that they felt God ought to keep them always on a high, and that they were endlessly on the mountain top, but life is not like that. And the Holy Spirit doesn't keep us always on a high.

Just because the Holy Spirit lives in you does not mean at all that you're going around all the time shouting, "Praise the Lord, praise the Lord!" There is nothing wrong with saying "Praise the Lord," but I suspect it ought to be used with discrimination. I met a young fellow not long ago who introduced himself to me, and I told him my name. He said, "Well, praise the Lord." Somehow I had a problem with that, for you see, hardly anyone I've ever seen could pronounce or spell my name the first time they heard it!

What I'm saying to you is: the Holy Spirit comes to live in us when we're born again, and he is there, the eternal presence of the living God in the lives of his children, and he makes available to us power for deliverance from sin. He doesn't immediately deliver us from it all, for that is a lifelong process. And that brings me to the second part of salvation.

Paul talked strangely about "work out your own salvation with fear and trembling." What was he talking about? He surely was not talking about the new birth. He said "for by grace are ye saved." That surely was not what he was talking about. He said, "I have not yet apprehended" after he had written a good part of the New Testament. He surely was not talking about being saved and being lost. That wasn't the emphasis of the apostle at all. He was talking about that continuing process which begins at the new birth in which the Holy Spirit in our lives constantly is working to help us finally become conformed to the image of Jesus Christ, God's Son. Of course, when we're saved, we're born again, our sins are forgiven, but sin continues to be a problem. Our lifelong habits may remain. Our afflictions continue to require the ministry of the Holy Spirit. Our ambitions continue to need the work of God day by day. Because of our ignorance of God's ways when we're born again, we need the constant instruction of the Holy Spirit of God in our lives all the time.

When I was a child our parents required us to memorize Scripture, and as we sat around the supper table every boy had to quote a passage of God's Word before we ate. And if you quoted the same passage three nights running, you had to memorize a new one before you got supper that night. But it's amazing how, after forty years, when Satan invades my heart and tries to take control of my life, the Spirit of God calls to mind the things that Jesus said and that I memorized out of the Word. And the Spirit of God with the Word condemns my temptation to sin. And if I stop to ask, he gives me power and strength to overcome it.

When the Christian is not overcoming sin, he is not living in submission to the Holy Spirit. When a Christian is constantly in the hot water of evil, it is because he is not listening to the voice of God in his heart as God works with him. When we are born anew, we are ignorant of God's ways; like a newborn babe in the world we are uncertain, insensitive to the Word of God. We are insensitive to the leadership of God in our lives, not knowing the Bible, not knowing what God has in store for us.

When the Holy Spirit enters our lives, just as babes we begin to grow little by little as the Holy Spirit instructs, as we learn to submit, as we learn new things about God, and as we learn how to avoid temptation and how to avoid sin by the power which God makes available to us through the Holy Spirit. Sin and evil everywhere plague us, but when we are born again, we begin the process of development as the children of God which includes the constant conscious elimination of evil. Our new life involves developing in the knowledge of Christ, the practice of the things of God, learning to surrender to God, and learning to serve God.

In other words, when one has been born again, he then begins the rest of his life, which is a life spent in becoming what God wants him to be. It is a lifelong pilgrimage. It is never finished until the very end. God, through the Holy Spirit, is helping us to become conformed to the image of Christ.

I don't know anybody who is yet conformed to the image of Christ, and yet God is working in our lives to do it. There are many ups and downs. Sometimes we feel like we're falling back as far as we're going forward. And I suspect sometimes we really are. Sin is that problem about which I talk, but the Book says, "If we confess our sins, he is faithful and just to forgive us *our* sins, and to cleanse us from all unrighteousness" (1 John 1:9).

What a remarkable thought that we do not as newborn children get cast out into the isolation of hell to be lost forever when we fall and fail. God says,"Repent, get up off of your face, go back to the life of living with Jesus Christ," and the life of the Christian is basically living out all of life's experiences with the person of Jesus Christ. But it is up and down.

In the Smoky Mountains there is a mountain called Mt. Mitchell. When my wife and I were on our honeymoon, we left Ridgecrest to take up our residence in New Orleans and to attend the seminary. We were coming back through the Smokies, and there was a sign that said something like "elevation 5,000 feet."

I was a country boy and she was raised in the mountains. Mountains were glorious to me, and we were in love and everything was glorious, anyway, and it still is. We came to a sign that directed us to Mt. Mitchell. My memory is that the sign said it's the highest spot east of the Mississippi River, 6,684 feet. Well, I had never seen anything as high as that. I wanted to see that mountain. And so we wound around the mountains, and we went up some and we went down some. It seemed that after about fifteen minutes we had been going down more than we were going up.

But we came to a sign which said "elevation 5,500 feet." And we went up some and down some and . . . I thought we were going down more than we were going up, but we came to a sign that read "elevation 6,000 feet." And shortly in one of those horseshoe turns we could look back far down the mountain and see the road up which we had driven. And finally we came to the end of the road, and there was a parking lot, and a sign nearby said something like "elevation 6,300 feet," but to reach the highest elevation, you had to *climb* up Mt. Mitchell.

Our lives as Christians are like that. It seems sometimes we make great progress and we rejoice, and other times it seems like we slide back, but it is a lifelong pilgrimage with Jesus Christ and we try to become what he wants us to be. When finally we come to the end of it, there is still some mountain up there we have not yet climbed, for we are not yet completely conformed to the image of Christ.

I'm so glad John wrote his first epistle. There's one verse in it that makes it all worthwhile. A verse that says, "Beloved, now are we the sons of God, and it doth not yet appear what we shall be: but we know that, when he shall appear, we shall be like him; for we shall see him as he is" (1 John 3:2). And there he's talking about glorification.

We have been justified by grace through faith. We are in the process of being sanctified by the work of the Holy Spirit in our lives, but, when at last we come to the end of the road, we will still be a long way from being conformed to the image of Christ. We will still be in the flesh. Our lives will still be unfinished. We will arrive at the gates of glory as unfinished products, for God will not yet have done all in us that he intends to do, but by his grace and mercy there we shall be conformed totally to the image of Christ. I can't imagine me being like Jesus, but he promised! We shall be like him.

This is our message to those who wander around confused and batter their heads on the rocks. The message is, "God will save you and God will change you and God will give you glory." And if that won't defeat hopelessness, there is no hope.

At the end of World War II we had put on board our ship a whole load of troops with their combat gear, with their tanks, guns, trucks, and ammunition. And the "scuttlebutt" (that's Navy for gossip) had it that we were going around the Horn to England. Other folks said, "No, you're going back to Japan with occupation troops again." And still other folks said, "No, you're taking these to China and there you will stand by for further orders."

That morning with the troops all on board, the lines had been singled up and we were ready to cast off. The bos'n's pipe shrilled through the squawk box and the bos'n's mate said, "Now hear this, now hear this, the captain of the ship." I'd been on it for months and months, and I had never before heard the captain on the squawk box. And he said, "This is Captain A. B. Leggett, United States Navy, commanding. We have received orders (I memorized what he said) from the United States Naval Department to proceed by the double great circle route to 'Uncle Sugar,' the United States."

I don't remember if the shout started with the black gang far down in the bowels of the ship, or with the troops on that five-inch number-one gun on the forward deck, or the troops on the fantail, or the watch in the crow's nest. But like the swell of the shouts of glory, we heard all over that ship, "Praise God, Hallelujah, praise

God, we're going home."

We went out past Corregidor and Bataan, and as we passed out between the island and the peninsula, Bataan as it reaches out toward Corregidor, I thought about what had transpired there. There stood by my side a hard-bitten army sergeant, and I noted that he was deeply moved. I made some comment to him about the "Bataan Death March" that had occurred there and the miseries that our troops had undergone.

He looked at me with tears in his eyes, and I knew this was unusual for he was an old army man, and he said "Yes, Chaplain, I know, I was there. Two hundred and twenty-something of us," he said, "went in; eight of us came out alive." And I could see the surge in his soul of the agony that he had lived through. All of those who lived through it and didn't die in it came back home with a guilt that they survived and others died. I could see it in his countenance that day, but then he smiled and said, "But thank God, we're going home."

Just outside the harbor of Manila we ran into one of the worst Pacific storms we had ever sailed in. Eight days and nights the ship went up and down. And ten days and nights she went back and forth. The sea was so rough that if you didn't brace yourself in the bunk, you would literally be tossed out on the steel deck.

We sat in the wardroom and held onto the table with one hand at 3 in the morning, drank coffee, and listened to the ship creak just forward of the number-three hold. And as we listened to her creak we received a message that a similar ship had broken in half during the same storm, and all hands aboard were lost.

And we prayed, "Oh God, just let this tub hold together for a few more days—we're going home." Some of the people on our ship had lived through the horrors of Okinawa. Kamikaze planes crashed into an ammunition ship very close by, and the horror of the scenes of fire and death in the explosions faded and receded into the distance. "Thank God, it's all done, the bombs are spilled. The plane engines roar only in peace, the dying is finished, and we have survived, and we're going home."

Oh, what a feeling! I recall the sun rising that morning between the twin peaks in San Francisco. I'll never forget it—it rose through the haze and the fog. As we sailed into the harbor, there came a yacht, and on that yacht was a band. It played all of the old songs that we sang in those days, and they shouted at us through megaphones "Welcome home! Welcome home!" I don't know if the girls on that yacht were as pretty as I thought they were, but they looked like angels. We warped into a pier in San Francisco harbor, and all around the bay there were signs in red, white, and blue: "Welcome Home."

My foot was the first one to touch the deck when the crew let the gangplank down. I think it's the only time I ever took advantage of the cross on my collar. I ran across to ring a telephone in Alameda across the bay. That voice I've loved since I was fifteen years old said, "Hello." And I had come home. We bought more flowers than the girls could wear and more candy than we could eat. I ate a whole head of lettuce at one sitting, I hadn't seen it in so long. We did all this just out of sheer joy to be back in a place where flowers grew. Where lettuce was available and where candy (not salt water chocolate) could be bought. Thank God we had come home!

One of these days He's going to say, "It's enough"—no terror for the Christian. No cold chilled waters of the Jordan for the believer. "I will come again and receive you unto myself that where I am there ye may be also." "And we shall be like him."

That is the message, and that's what those troubled, hurting people need. God is available in Jesus Christ.

8
The Moment of Truth

It may well be that when the history of twentieth-century Christianity is written, many of you will be able to say, "I was there when God did his great work."

These have been exciting days, a time when a body of believers called Southern Baptists have systematically proceeded from commission to concept to challenge—and hopefully now, commitment. This has been the era when the Convention rose and asked its agencies, "We want the most challenging evangelistic and missionary program in the history of faith." These have been the days when the Home Mission Board has voiced to America, "We want every person in the confines of the land to hear the gospel by the year 2000." This has been the time when the Foreign Mission Board has systematically probed the frontiers of the earth and has come back to report, "There are billions out there who have never heard the name of Christ."

We have lived in a time when God, anticipating the fulfillment of his purpose, has called multiplied thousands of young people and filled our colleges, universities, and seminaries when we did not even know that we needed them. These have been years filled with fevered meetings, endless committees, plans, projects, programs, and projections. In an unparalleled action, the denomination's executive committee requested the rewriting of the program emphases for years to come. State convention structures have adjusted their budgets and their methods of operation, gearing for an effort unknown in our history.

Volunteers by the score are being identified for the Mission Service Corps, and the Home Mission Board has already identified in this country more than one thousand places where a Mission Service Corps volunteer is needed. A new concept in mission information delivery has been born, and all of the appropriate agencies of Southern Baptists have teams hard at work trying to make sure that every Baptist in the land knows about the mission and evangelistic opportunities of the day. The evangelical world is alert to the fact that Southern Baptists are getting serious about the commission of Christ. One noted religious leader has said, "Hope for religious awakening in our time lies with Southern Baptists and the Bold Mission effort."

Charles Cappleman, a Methodist layman who is general manager of CBS Television City in Hollywood, has made some observations concerning the church and its communications:

". . . I find that the evangelistic zeal is missing in many of our mainline Protestant churches. . . . Mainline Protestant churches appear to be on the defensive and are losing membership. . . . As much as our churches are short of funds, it seems to me that we are more short of creativity. There is more we could do with what we have. . ."

And although Southern Baptists may not be considered by some a mainline denomination, here is the challenge of Bold Mission Thrust: creativity—doing more with what we have.

Never have there been so many trumpet sounds of advance, so much shuffling of the paper, so many meetings of the committees, or so many reams of paper devoted to an effort. And now, at last, we come to the moment of truth. The dust is settling and after the meeting of the 1978 Convention the strident noises of an army girding for war will begin to die. Routines in the denomination at every level must be reestablished in the interest of the ongoing work. The decisions are made, the committees have met, the differences have been resolved; all the denominational organizations, mechanisms, institutions and programs are in place, and we stand at the moment of truth.

Now it comes down to you and me and our churches. It won't matter now that we claim to be orthodox, for theology will not be enough. "Faith without works is dead," and the issue is clearly drawn. It won't be enough to preach sermons and give devotions. It won't be enough to do art work, run the mimeograph machine, teach mission study books, and talk to other people about what is involved. When the inspiration of all our meetings fades like rose petals from yesterday's bouquets, the issue will still come down to you and me.

Some of the issues, as we face these crucial days, are crystal clear. Is the commission of Christ to the church authoritative for us?

The whole commission of our Lord is predicated on the fact that persons without faith in Jesus Christ are lost. They are lost in time. They are lost in eternity. It may well be that Southern Baptists are not nearly as orthodox on this point as we would like our critics to believe. We have been culturally conditioned by creeping universalism that is not taught, but caught. The oft-repeated statements of our world are sometimes accepted as fact. When it is said, "They have a culture; we have no right to try to change them," multitudes have begun to believe that. When it has been said that this is the post-missionary era and that the old-fashioned way of leading people from their native religious ideas to our own has outlived its usefulness, I am afraid that idea has some converts among us. It is not enough that we repeat the theological *shibboleths.* It is mandatory that we face the truth about the condition of persons without Christ, however bright, attractive, cultured, refined, or rich they may be. People without God are lost.

As we think about the nature of the authoritative commission, we must ask ourselves anew the questions, "Is the desperate evil everywhere around us the legitimate concern of Christians and churches?" "Is it serious or fatal for people to be in rebellion against God?" "Do we really believe that the natural mind of man is enmity against God?" "Do we really believe that man is the victim of a fatal malady that will destroy him, his family, and his society if it goes unchecked?"

The desperate evil of immorality, of sexual abuse and perversion, of the abuse of families, the disintegration of the home, of the escapist society, of a crime burden that blankets the country—these are concerns about desperate evil, and the commission of Christ is directly applicable to them.

The Scriptures present the church as God's people living in a hostile world. We are to be in the world but not of the world: a catalyst, a conscience, a castigator of evil, a people whose very presence is a condemnation of evil.

If our values are not different from those of the world, we are not worthy of being called the people of God. The Scriptures present us as the body of Christ in the world. It is an astonishing thought that we are supposed to be the embodied representatives of Jesus Christ in this alien world. Is it his purpose that we shall consume his bounty, his love, and his grace upon ourselves, or that we shall be light reflectors or irritating, but curing, salt? Will we settle in these times for a cultural conformity and for the comfort of a compatible church? Will we simply slough off the commission of Christ by contenting ourselves with trying to develop quality and forgetting the quantity of persons who are hurting and lost?

When all the shouting dies out, and the sounds of a muted trumpet in the distance echo, will we settle back into the same old rut? Or will you and I assume the responsibility for becoming an evangelistic and missionary force in our town, on our street, in our country, and throughout the world? Did Christ really mean it when he stressed, "Ye shall be my witnesses"?

Another of the issues which should be clear to us is formulated in the question, Is the plight of the persons we know of concern to us? Do we care about all these people? Does it mean anything to us that, as the Father sent Christ to us in our hurt, our loneliness, our sorrow, our confusion, our sins, he in turn has sent us to people in the same condition?

Some time ago, I was at a meeting in a certain state. The director of the child-care program in that state drove my wife Bettye and me to the airport. He began talking to us about the plight of the children with whom he dealt. He told us, for example, that last year in his state 180 children were born to preteenage girls. He noted that one half of all the children in his state born last year were illegitimate. He explained that the majority of the girls with which they dealt (there were hundreds of them) were victims of rape, incest, or molestation.

About us there are millions of dislocated, disfranchised children; children who have no future outside the love of God. These are children for whom few seem to care. These are the children who are the citizens of tomorrow. They are the children for whom Christ died and for whom you and I are responsible.

Not very long ago, in a large southern city, a pastor and I were walking down the church hallway, when the child-care director saw us and stepped out to visit with us. As the pastor introduced us, the director found out that I was from the Sunday School Board. She asked me a question, "What would you do," she said, "if a mother brought a beautiful six-month-old infant in to you, placed that beautiful baby in your arms, and said, 'Here he is; he was unexpected; he is unwanted; and he is unloved. See what you can do for this brat'?"

Here was a child who is defeated before he can even sit up, disowned before he can walk, and emotionally insecure before he can speak. What if someone doesn't love him? What if someone doesn't bring him to understand that God loves him? America is full of them. The same kinds of things can be said about the young adults who struggle with the problems of life, who are seeking ways out of the pressures which have beset them, who are seeking meaning to otherwise colorless, dull, gray lives. The same could be said for those who finish a career. The children are gone. Life holds no sweetness. There is no purpose. There is no tomorrow.

As I think about those with whom we are associated in our streets and in our towns, I also think about the teeming millions of Los Angeles County, for instance. More than half of them have skin that doesn't look like mine. Millions of them speak with an accent that doesn't sound like my Southern drawl. Many of them have come from the far stretches of the earth, seeking in this land a livelihood when what they really need is the *abundant life.*

It is surely selfish to think only of those in our land when I can remember the tramping hordes on the streets of Tokyo, Hong Kong, and Manila; the shy and hesitant tribesmen from the African back country, the dark eyes and dull faces of the peasants high in the Andes. These are no demographic statistics; these are persons, persons for whom Jesus Christ died. The basic issue for you and me is: Will we in our time, given the comfort of our homes, the security of our families, the relative ease of our livelihoods, force ourselves out of the lethargy of self-satisfaction and plenty to share our time, ourselves, and our substance with these persons who hurt and die, who long and hate, and live and love—people for whom Jesus Christ died? The issue now is not what will the denomination say or what will the agencies plan; the issue now is, What will you and I do?

Other questions that we are confronted with are: Will I find purpose as a Christian? Will I invest my life in what God is doing in the earth?

Whether or not we like it, whether or not we admit it, and whether or not we're prepared to accept the consequences, the nature of our lives is eternally important. Whatever we do or don't do has eternal consequences. What we do lives. What we do reproduces after its kind. What we do multiplies as it impacts the lives of others.

It is not enough merely to be a churchgoer or a lip server or an orthodox believer when we consider all that gross evil that threatens to inundate our society.

This is the hour when the people of God must fulfill God's purpose in our lives instead of being one of those who sits and waits. There is an unprecedented demand that we become a part of the sweep of the grace of God, that we take our places in the tidal flow of God's love and let it spread across the entire world. The Word of God makes it abundantly clear that God calls all of us, not only to righteousness, but he calls us to serve in his work in the ways he makes possible and fruitful.

All of this comes down to this question: Will my church and I be comfortable simply to melt into the society and culture while America struggles, gasps, and dies, and while the world stands on the brink of an unparalleled holocaust? For us, of necessity, the appropriate Christian response is, "I will personally take my place as a sharer of the gospel." I'm well aware of the age-worn excuse, "But I can't speak well," or "I don't know how to witness." Perhaps this is true, but every one of us has the capacity to speak or write in order to share what God has done for us. The New Testament is full of the testimonies of those who were saying to others, "This is what God has done for me." This is something every one of us can do. It does not matter what else we do—if somehow we do not become sharers of the gospel, we will not be fulfilling the command of Christ for us.

Every one of us can become a leader for evangelism and missions in our church. We're all familiar with the old saying, "There are those who watch things happen, there are those who make things happen, and there are those who don't know what has happened."

If ever there was a time when Southern Baptists should rise *en masse* in our churches and demand an ongoing program of evangelism and missions, this is that time. Every pastor I know, and I know thousands, would rejoice if there were an uprising in his congregation from the people saying, "Pastor, we must come to grips with our evangelistic opportunity, and we must do something about the mission obligation that is thrust upon us." There is no way to know what the people who read this could do if we all went home and said, "We must do more than we've ever done before."

A third way we can invest our lives in that which is eternally significant is to become a sharer with the unsaved of God's bounty to us. If we simply tithed, we would be giving approximately five times more to the propagation of the gospel than we are. If our churches only tithed through the Cooperative Program, we would vastly increase the financial resources the mission boards are waiting to receive in order to do the job.

There is one part of our polity that really fences us in and hems us up to the truth about God's work and about ourselves. We have long proclaimed that we believe in the priesthood of all believers; this means freedom and the ability to decide for ourselves what we will do. No one can assess us to give money; no one can require ecclesiastical performance. Our churches enjoy free and autonomous existence.

What we often fail to realize is that the other side of this coin makes us responsible for response to the leading of Christ. If we're free to choose and to respond to God, and it is an individual matter, this means ultimate responsibility for me and my church in implementing the command of Christ. It does not matter what anyone else does. Christian faith requires that we accept the responsibility for personal response to Christ and to his commission to the church. This responsibility holds regardless of what anyone else does, regardless of what anyone else says, and whether or not the people in my church agree with what I believe. I am ultimately responsible for sharing my life for the eternal purposes of God.

Here is the chance to let your life take on an eternal purpose. Here is a way that you can live significantly now. Here is a way that your influence can live on forever. Here is a way you can join in the sweep of what God is doing in the world whether anyone else does. Regardless of success or failure, you as an individual child of God are responsible to him for yourself, and you and your fellow believers are responsible for your church. Here is your grandest hour.

One mission quote from across many years still sticks like a burr in my mind. One of the mission heroes once said, "I have seen in the light of the morning sun, the rooftops of a thousand villages where the name of Christ has never been heard."

As I have flown back and forth across this land, up and down its length and across its breadth, and to scores of places across the earth, I have stared into the eyes of thousands of faces that do not know Christ, and I have seen the lights of a million homes where his name is not known or honored.

I have seen the millions, and I have heard their cry. I have looked at the children and felt their wants. I have gazed into the eyes of those who have grown tired and gray, and I have known something of the sorrow and the aching emptiness that besets them.

I have seen the vitality of the young consumed

upon themselves, upon fads, and upon that which endures not . . . and I challenge you, my fellow Baptists, this is our time, this our hour, this is our chance to proclaim *unto all the world.* "For God so loved the world, that he gave his only begotten Son, that whosoever believeth in him should not perish, but have everlasting life" (John 3:16). Let us say, you and I, "We have come to show you that love of God in the showcase of the human heart."